C000160525

In Another W

—

Also by Tom Pow

In Another World

—

Among Europe's Dying Villages

Polygon

First published in Great Britain in 2012 by Polygon, an imprint of Birlinn Ltd, West Newington House, 10 Newington Road, Edinburgh EH9 1QS
www.polygonbooks.co.uk

Copyright © 2012, Tom Pow. Images © 2012, Tom Pow

The right of Tom Pow to be identified as the author of this work has been asserted in accordance with the Copyright, Design and Patent Act 1988.

All rights reserved. No part of this publication may be reproduced, stored, or transmitted in any form, or by any means, electronic, mechanical or photocopying, recording or otherwise, without the express written permission of the publisher.

ISBN: 978 1 84697 195 2
British Library Cataloguing-in-Publication Data
A catalogue record for this book is available on request from the British Library.

The extract from 'The Village' by Iain Crichton Smith, published in *Collected Poems* (1992), is reprinted by kind permission of Carcanet Press Limited. The extract from 'The Tale the Hermit Told' by Alastair Reid, published in *Inside Out: Selected Poems and Translations* (Polygon, 2008), is reprinted by kind permission of the author. The extract from 'New Space' by Derek Mahon, published in *An Autumn Wind* (2010), is reprinted by kind permission of the author and The Gallery Press, Loughcrew, Oldcastle, County Meath, Ireland. The three extracts from *Russian Folklore* by Y. M. Sokolov (translated by Catherine Ruth Smith; 2011) are reprinted by kind permission of Wildside Press.

The editor and publisher gratefully acknowledge the permission granted to reproduce the copyright material in this book. Every effort has been made to trace copyright holders and to obtain their permission for the use of copyright material. If there are any errors or omissions the publisher would be grateful if notified of any corrections that should be incorporated in future reprints or editions of this book.

The publisher acknowledges investment from Creative Scotland towards the publication of this volume.

Text design by Teresa Monachino.
Printed and bound by T J International, Padstow, Cornwall.

for
Julie,
Cameron and Jenny

and for
Alistair Moffat

Author's Note

In 2007, I received a Creative Scotland Award from the Scottish Arts Council to respond to the phenomenon of dying villages in Europe. I visited some of the areas most deeply affected by depopulation and I responded in the ways my imagination prompted me. It has been an ongoing project and some of the material in this book has appeared in other forms. There have been three chapbooks: *Songs from a Dying Village, Ceann Loch Reasort and Other Dead Village Walks* and *The Village and the Road*, which has translations into Spanish by Mike Gonzalez and Marianella Yanes. There has also been a book of photographs, *Sites of Loss*, and a website, *www.dyingvillages.com*. Several of the poems were published in *New Walk*, while 'Walnut Gatherers' was first published in *In The Becoming, New and Selected Poems* (Polygon 2009). I have given several talks on the subject, one of which was published in *The Scottish Review of Books* under the title (not mine) 'Villages of the Damned'. I am grateful to Vittoria Hancock for alerting me, during a workshop I gave on 'The Village and the Road' at the Scottish Storytelling Centre, to the concept of *hiraeth* and for her translation of the ancient Welsh folksong. I am equally indebted to Marian Angeles Huarte for the miraculous transcribing of some Spanish drinking songs, recorded far into the wee hours. The short extracts from Pierre Jourde's *Pays Perdu* (L'Esprit des Péninsules, Paris, 2006) were translated by me. I would also like to acknowledge a debt to *Human Cargo* by Caroline Moorhead (Chatto and Windus, London, 2005), which I found invaluable in writing the story 'The Gift from the Sea'.

A book that has several journeys running through it is one that owes a great debt of thanks to a large number of people – interviewees, hosts, conversationalists and photographic subjects. My interpreter, Maria (Masha) Nikolaeva, was an invaluable source of support to me in Russia, while Helen Pearson, lately of Border Television, brought energy and ingenuity to a short film she made there about the project. My thanks extend to *all* who appear within these covers, but also to all those who don't – people who gave their time and their reactions and enthusiasm throughout the length of this project. Among many, I recall a lively, early discussion with Joanna Kelly, an ex-pupil of mine now based in Lyon. And, in talking of enthusiasm and support, I could not forget to thank my agent, Jenny Brown.

This is the third of my books for which Mike Gonzalez has been first line editor. He has been informed, responsive, helpful and professional on each occasion. I am also immensely grateful to the editing skills of my in-house editor, Sarah Ream. I had always thought, within each travel book, that there are two journeys – the actual journey and then the writing of it. Sarah has taught me that, in certain cases, there are three – the last one is the editing process. It is at this stage that the book becomes itself. I want to thank Sarah for the sensitivity, the sympathy and the bristling intelligence she brought to the task, while accepting sole responsibility for the result. I have the director of Polygon, Neville Moir, to thank for Sarah: my thanks to him, Hugh Andrew and all at Polygon and Birlinn for the professional way they have undertaken the production of *In Another World*. I knew from the start that design would be an essential element of the book and thank Teresa Monachino for her sensitivity and James Hutcheson for persevering till we arrived at a cover with which we were all happy.

Alistair Moffat produces books with bewildering speed. I do not, and so he must share the dedication with my family. He will know that does not lessen the love and affection behind the gesture. My family are my travelling companions, and sometimes I lead them down long and twisting roads. How lucky am I that my wife, Julie, who carries the heaviest (metaphorical) pack, never urges me to turn back.

Tom Pow
Dumfries 2012

Contents

A man and a woman once sat down
at a bare table and looked out
at the sky. What needs to be done?

they asked, so that, in later years,
their children or their grandchildren
might ask, What shall we do today?

In Another World: *Among Europe's Dying Villages*

Prologue: Withering Heights

There were three roads
*   out of the village –*
two led into the world;
*   the other to the sky*

Now each of these roads
*   has been taken,*
the village spins
*   uselessly in the wind*

I woke early, ragged and jet-lagged, in my hotel room in the heart of the Canadian Prairies. I put on a tracksuit and trainers and went outside into the lightly falling snow to run away the lethargy and to take advantage of the conjunction of memory and the moment. I had been invited back to Edmonton, where I had lived for a year thirteen years earlier, to celebrate thirty years of the Writing Program at the University of Alberta. Block by block, I felt my way back into the city – its broad streets, the concrete and glass bulwarks of its university, the trees that mark the sides of the valley where the North Saskatchewan River flows. An old dog sniffing for something that smells like a trail.

Edmonton is still a young city. First established as a trading post, Fort Edmonton, in 1795, it has been state capital for just over one hundred years. Its historic main street, Whyte Avenue, still has the low-horizon, sidewalk feel of a street that could be as long as it wanted to be, given the material and the labour available. But, away from this vertebra and its ribs, Edmonton is an oil-rich city designed for the car. Broad boulevards lead to its downtown areas, mirror-bright and metallic, while its spreading suburbs – clapboard houses with neat lawns – follow a grid system.

From a base at Edmonton, a little over a hundred years ago, immigrant settlers moved north. Their labour and their loneliness still feel immense, their severing of contact with 'the old country' heartbreakingly acute. Many of their namings, shorn of their native rhythms, read like perfunctory tags – Peace River, Wandering River, Slave Lake. The landscape was too vast, their creative energy too limited, their knowledge too slight to conjure anything but the most basic resonance. Enormous space still surrounds the settled land, though towns – ones with names like these – thrive in the emptiness.

Ironically, many of the experiences that came out of the individual's struggle for survival are communal ones that bind Canadians and have influenced their strongly democratic traditions. In *The Company of Adventurers*, Peter C. Newman suggested that it was the wide-ranging commercial endeavours of the Hudson Bay Company that had created Canada's geographical unity. In addition, in the 1800s, over half the able-bodied men in Canada had supplemented their incomes by spending winter in a logging camp. This seasonal work transformed the lives of almost every Canadian family and gave them a shared experience almost as common as war.

Canadian writing still acknowledges and draws on its closeness to the natural world in a way that few other literatures do. In *Survival*, her thematic guide to Canadian literature, Margaret Atwood once tethered Canadian literature to an image of scribbling on the marginalia of the pressing wilderness, ever at risk of oblivion. And though many contemporary writers resent what they see as a backward-looking perspective, others show an awareness of how brief their presence has been in the Canadian landscape.

The Saskatchewan poet, Tim Lilburn, one of those celebrants at the University of Alberta, addresses such concerns in his essay 'Philosophical Apokatastasis: On Writing and Return': 'We aren't from where we are; we, descendants of European settlers, don't come from this ground,' he writes. 'We have our graves here; we have spent a few generations changing the land but [. . .] landscapes have long, exacting apprenticeships and in the aspen country of north central Saskatchewan and in the grassland south of it Cree, Assiniboine, Lakota, Saulteux and others have finished theirs.'

¶

Thick shavings of snow fell on my face. I brushed them away and kept my head tilted to the pavement, finding a track through the snow. The Sunday streets were quiet. At one intersection, a car pulled back its snout to let me pass, an accommodation that, through the shrouding snow, reconnected me with what I once knew of this city and its inhabitants, gentlemen of the Prairies.

Later, showered, awake, I sat in the Second Cup, a corner café on Whyte Avenue. Perched on a high stool, I looked out of the window and could almost see my wife Julie in her black poncho and multi-coloured scarf as she pushed Cameron in his buggy, his hands clutching onto Blue Bunny.

'You look lost in thought there, buddy,' said a waitress – with a characteristic lightness that again sounded a note in my memory.

'Yes, I, we, used to come here thirteen years ago with our son.' And I heard my voice sounding reedy and cracked.

I sipped my Java and opened that day's *Edmonton Journal*, a broadsheet with a comfortable, roomy feel to it, and it brought me back to a familiarity that wasn't freighted with emotion. In its pages, I once read reviews of writers whose names hadn't crossed the state boundary, let alone the pond, and I had enjoyed the detachment and grace of the literary outsider. In its 'Sunday Reader' section this morning was a front-page article with the title 'Withering Heights', concerning 'The dozen citizens still living in Villabandin, Spain – who range in age from 58 to 91 – [who] cannot clearly recall the last wedding or christening in their dying village.' There was a photograph of a severe-looking old woman, in the stiffness of a pose: 'Milagros Garcia, an eighty-year-old widow, pauses in reflection after gathering some eggs from the farmyard.'

On the inside, a spread of photographs showed the village – a grey clutch of roofs – alongside pictures of its church and its twelve permanent inhabitants. 'Who will look after our graves, once we are gone?' one of them asked. 'After us there will be nothing.' The article explained that the experience of Villabandin in Castile and León was replicated in many other parts of Spain and across Europe, from Portugal to Russia.

I felt a jolt of recognition as one place brought to mind others from other times, each sitting inside the other, like a set of Russian dolls. The images of Spanish depopulation that contrasted with the bright, wooden, New World structures of Edmonton brought to mind the stubborn remains from the part of Scotland where my template of abandonment first took root – to where, whenever I am faced with a domestic ruin, my imagination returns. Even standing below a lintel in a house at Machu Picchu, breathing in a familiar smell of damp moss and fern, it had been the resonance of a deserted croft house in Scotland that I had felt.

¶

For much of my childhood and early adulthood, my parents owned a cottage in the northeastern Highlands of Scotland. It stood at a slight distance from the village of Culrain, which itself lies a few miles from Bonar Bridge, the portal for the main artery north until the bridge was built at Dornoch. We started going there in the sixties, around the time people were talking about the A9 north as 'the Road to Nowhere' and when the famous newspaper headline had appeared asking the 'Last person to leave the Highlands [to] switch off the lights.'

The cottage had been filled with hay bales when my father offered to buy it from the farmer, the pair of them bargaining in the field where it stood. The village itself – with the whitewashed farm as its centrepiece – stood close to the dismal pond into which (it is alleged) James Graham, First Marquis of Montrose, leader of a doomed uprising on behalf of the Stuart king, cast his armour after his final defeat on 27 April 1650. The pond's name was Loch Sprint, but it was not so much a loch as the undrained sump of one, surrounded by a few straggly trees. It was a location, in other words, without romance or sentiment. And yet, such is the Scots twinning of glory with defeat, I found it perfectly possible to imagine handsome Montrose's armour preserved and shining in its gloopy depths.

The village had once served Carbisdale Castle, now a youth hostel but, at the start of its history, a vivid example of the combination of

In Another World: *Among Europe's Dying Villages*

power and pique. The castle (built 1907–1917), the local story went, had been strategically placed on a raised promontory, overlooking the Kyle of Sutherland, by the dowager Duchess of Sutherland to mark more intensely her disapproval of her son's marriage. His private railway was routed below the castle, and, when he was passing, the duchess ordered all curtains on that side of her baronial heap to be closed.

From the top of Struie Hill – a good ten miles away – your eye is led to the distant castle as surely as it would be in any Renaissance landscape. There is indeed every measure of Highland grandeur in this 'million dollar view', but, closer in, up the straths and the glens, I used to feel an ineffable sadness. If, for example, you continued the road up Strath Oykel, which, until relatively recently, led to a dead end, you would see the broken shells of croft houses from the clearances, their abandonment and ruin only highlighted by the few intermittent white bungalows or renovations.

Even more poignantly, at the head of the glen of Strathcarron, stands Croick Church. Here had been one of the most infamous illustrations of the callous nature of the clearances. Those cleared from Glencalvie had seen themselves not as victims of oppression but of God-given laws: 'Glencalvie people the wicked generation', one of them had scratched on a window of the church they had felt unworthy to enter, sheltering instead below the raised gravestones in its grounds. More pertinently, another had written, 'Murder was in the year 1845'.

'If such as happened here transpired in the south, there would be outrage,' wrote an anonymous reporter from *The Times* on 2 June 1845 with an indignation that was unable to affect change. It was hard not to see those who survived on the clearance lands as profoundly marked by their inheritance. In the years of my deepest acquaintance with the Highlands, I often felt there to be something reserved and separate about those who lived there, something guarded that went beyond the usual reticence of country people. It was as if they had tasted a defeat that still made them wary. I would say these might have been the reactions of a young, over-sensitive mind, if it were not that along every strath and glen lay the stone evidence of abandonment and death.

Prologue: Withering Heights

This living and tangible inheritance of defeat is one that is missing from southwest Scotland, where I have lived for the past thirty-five years. The story of its clearances is only now being fully researched and told. But these are early days for a public appreciation of the fact that the three counties of Dumfriesshire, Kirkcudbrightshire and Wigtownshire experienced proportionately greater loss from emigration in the nineteenth century than did the clearance counties in the Highlands. The reasons for this untold story are various. The nature of the two clearances differed – the lowland one was connected with enclosure and agricultural 'improvement'. The ruination of the cottar dwellings was a matter of coercion into a wholly different social and agricultural arrangement; 'removal' was the term used, rather than the more emotive 'clearance'. There was also, at that time, no media coverage able to communicate the hardships of the people. Neither is there the clearly visible legacy of loss that the Highlands still displays, as most of the lowland stone was incorporated into new builds or into dykes. But perhaps, most crucially, the southwest did not have the same build-up to its clearances as the Highlands, which witnessed the crushing defeat of Culloden and the systematic, attempted dismantling of a living, cohesive culture, one whose language has been fighting for oxygen and speakers ever since. Moreover, in the Highlands, the clan chiefs, acting as distant landowners and military entrepreneurs, ensured a sense of betrayal that would resonate from generation to generation.

There is, though, a sense in which the Highlands and the southwest of Scotland share common challenges – ones which relate to the problem of maintaining the village as a community with a shared sense of purpose against a backcloth of demographic decline. Throughout Scotland, Scotland's Rural Past, a recent lottery-funded initiative (2006–2011), has done much to investigate and to help us to re-imagine our rich rural past. It has achieved this by empowering communities 'to research, record and promote Scotland's vanishing historic rural settlements and landscapes'. Much of the evidence here was ignored by the first Ordnance Survey mapmakers. All mapmakers have their own strictures: theirs was not to record any buildings post 1750 or any ruin that did not reach knee height.

The *ferm toun* settlement of Polmaddy in the Galloway Forest, which was abandoned in the early nineteenth century, was one of Scotland's Rural Past's instructional sites. On an induction tour, an archaeologist pointed out the broken walls that had been the inn and led the group between the stone foundations that had once been an alleyway between a tight knot of houses. He showed us the gap-toothed evidence of where a cruck barn's supports had been slotted and where the footings of a corn-drying kiln had been set. There is always an excitement in re-imagining lives in this way. But what is the pull of a deserted site – or of a site that is clearly dying? There is the sense of absence certainly:

> the headlands
>   which wail of exiles,
>   the stiles
> over which ghosts leap
>   like angels

(from section 29 of 'The Village' by Iain Crichton Smith)

And there is also something compelling about the limitations which geography once imposed on the lives lived there, a constriction that was intimately concerned with the meaning of home. In his meditation, *And our faces, my heart, brief as photos*, John Berger argues that home was, at one time, at the centre of two intersecting lines: a vertical line, leading both to heaven and to the underworld, and a horizontal one, which represented, 'the traffic of the world, all the possible roads leading across the world to other places'. Such centredness, once a given, is a rarity in the twenty-first century. Now 'the new nomads', as Eva Hoffman describes them in her essay of the same name, are 'Don Juans of experience who travel perpetually to new movements and sensations and to whom no internal site – of attachment, need, desire – is more important than any other.'

¶

Prologue: Withering Heights

I have lived through a time of demographic decline, one predicted in Scotland's rural areas to worsen: in the 2009 election one in three voters in Scotland's southwest was a pensioner. In such fragile circumstances, a village needs a sense of itself and a shared purpose to survive. In Scotland and elsewhere on the European continent, many villages are being transformed from what they were. In some cases, such villages – for example, those around property-rich cities like Edinburgh and Pamplona – reflect the gentrification of the countryside, as villages become dormitories for the city.

In his *Villages of Britain*, Clive Aslet takes a relaxed view of such developments: 'Many English villages began as dormitories. They put roofs over the heads of the families who toiled on the lord's fields and kept his sheep, managed his woods or dug his mines.' He comments that 'The great village industries of today are tourism and retirement, with much of the village population commuting to jobs elsewhere.' That 'the village has once more transformed itself [. . .] is nothing new.'

However, the villages that excited my imagination from my stool in the Second Cup were not those that had reached a comfortable accommodation with change and circumstance. My interests, I felt, would lead me to those that were the last of their kind, lying at Berger's intersections of spiritual and worldly traffic, or to places that could not be re-invented or renewed without great challenges.

I was already aware that the complex situation of a village holding onto a sense of its past, while trying to imagine a future, presents narrative challenges different from those of villages which are, visibly and emphatically, dying. Filmmaker Alex Barclay and I had worked together on a creative arts project centred on the village of Ae. Named after the water that flows below it, Ae lies at the head of a valley, some ten miles north of Dumfries. Our purpose there was to help the ten pupils from the primary school, the school staff and the villagers to tell stories about the past, to record the present and to create memories for the future. Ae was the first of Scotland's forty forest villages built after the war to keep people in the countryside and to attract them to it. The initial plan for the village was more ambitious than the one that was eventually built, but it still had a school, a village hall, a shop and a post office.

As a girl of seven, in 1949, Margaret Finlay moved into house number one in Ae. A newspaper headline above a photograph of her family group – mother with tin basin underarm, father with a mound of bedding – announced, 'A New Name Goes on the Map of Scotland'. Below the photograph, another heading proclaimed, 'A Turnip Lantern Lights the Way'. Handy that Margaret should be carrying one, as there was no electricity in the house. That would come later and increase the rent by two pounds per year.

The planned village, with its shared inception, offers a very particular kind of community experience. Nevertheless, it holds true that, nowadays, the community identity of villages is not born out of necessity, as it once was, but out of choice, and it is made up of many strands – one of which will most likely be the common destination used for work, shopping or leisure; a reminder that it has been the car as much as anything that has changed our (village) communities. But it is also highly possible that one of these strands will be a sense of absence.

'Over a hundred men,' Davie King told me, 'once worked in the forest here. Two buses brought men out from Dumfries and there were others who got here under their own steam.'

'I mind seeing them,' said Frank Cook, 'in the morning striding out from the village down to the forest. They were like an army. I can't remember them saluting, though, except when they got paid. They queued for their pay – alphabetically. A great long line of them.'

The village hall was the centre of village life then. 'There was something on every night,' said Davie. 'Bowling, drama, dancing – the only thing we didn't do was badminton because the roof was too low.' But then along came television.

Again, I am drawn to consider communities in the northwest of Scotland, part of whose present identity, for those who live there, might be composed of a number of elements: the absence of those removed through emigration and clearance; the stories of those who have injected the community with welcome or unwelcome new life;

and a shared culture that may include traditional music, contemporary crafts and, in the case of Lochinver certainly, the poems of Norman MacCaig. The plaiting of such seemingly disparate narratives is one way, as Tim Lilburn puts it in his essay 'How To Be Here?', 'to find our way to take the place in our mouth [. . .] to re-say our past in such a way that it will gather us here'.

Concerns with memory, home, love lost and mourned, elegy, earth and stone. This is the material out of which I have always made my poems and stories. Reading about the 'Withering Heights' on the other side of the world, I had the sense of Europe as a totality; the landmass on the planet I knew most fully, the one I had crossed and recrossed by thumb, rail, bus, train and car. I imagined a permeable lining falling from it and the whole continent becoming irrevocably changed.

Islanders

At the other side
of the world, they remembered.
Playing pool, say, or reaching
for a bat. Some memory
came back of what their fathers
or grandfathers had told them.

Their hands were still reaching
for tools, still feeling a need
to make a world – though now
it was all there before them
if they only put in the hours.

As the dead village became
a museum, this other village lived on
in them. In their neighbourhoods
they nodded curtly, as their forebears had,
coming up, laden, from the strand.
In the great clouds they welcomed
the white rollers crashing in.

PART ONE

The Village and the Road

The Village and the Road

There are those on the road who never think
of the village
    There are those in the village
who have made their lives an open road

1

At about five in the afternoon, I began the walk from Murias de Paredes to Villabandin. Both villages lie in the region of Omaña, one of the most sparsely populated parts of Europe. Villabandin itself is situated on a loop, around fifteen kilometres away from the 'main' road, which crosses Omaña from La Magdalena to the mining town of Villablino. You must make a deliberate choice to go there, and few do; only one car passed me on my journey. On the roadside leaving Murias, there was a dead snake, coiled and drying, but everywhere else the land was full of life, *floreciente*. I walked alongside a gurgling stream – the signature sound of each village I would visit.

From the crossroads at Senira, the road rose towards the village of Lazado. The shimmering birches that had flanked the road until then gave way to a more open landscape of pasture and scrub. Three caramel-coated cows, their bells ringing richly and deeply, stood at the fountain in Lazado. In their own time, they made way for that one car. Then there was silence on the road again, a stillness broken only by a distant bell, an occasional lowing, birdsong. Casting my eyes away from the lowering sun, I saw a giant flying ant flailing on the road. Its silvery fairy wings were enormous, ungainly out of the air; I watched it being carried off by road ants.

It is good to walk out on an open road, to breathe in the summer smells of fresh-cut hay and cow shit. Good to be unencumbered and to be excited by what one will find. Villages of course often draw themselves in against those from the open road – the drifters and vagabonds that the French were constantly legislating against throughout the eighteenth and nineteenth centuries. But, in kinder times, it is hard not to associate an edge of romance with such wanderers. Certainly, nineteen-year-old Laurie Lee, walking out one midsummer morning in 1934 and landing at Vigo, felt himself open up to what a drifting life on the road had to offer:

> I had skirted the mountains of Leon, coming through shaded oak-woods and groves of figs and almond, along great shelves of rock where wooden ox-carts laboured and boys in broad hats went leaping up the hillsides pursuing their scattered flocks. I'd come through poor stone villages, full of wind and dust, where mobs of children convoyed me through the streets, and where priests and women quickly crossed themselves when they saw me, and there was nothing to buy except sunflower seeds.

Laurie Lee's *As I Walked Out One Midsummer Morning* describes a journey framed by the village and the road. But, however much I felt like (a considerably older) Laurie Lee, the village I was walking towards had been utterly changed since Lee's travels in Spain.

In the next thirty years, Europe will lose almost one third of its population. Rural areas will be most affected. Trends such as low birth rates, growing numbers of elderly people and high levels of emigration as young people head for the city have already transformed large parts of rural Spain, France, Italy and Germany in the most significant demographic changes since the Black Death wiped out as much as two thirds of Europe's population in the late 1340s. The most recent census found that around a hundred of Spain's 5,000 villages are facing imminent extinction. Moreover, demographic decline is not limited to the areas of central and southern Europe to which I travelled. Areas in northern Europe are similarly affected. In Sweden, for example, eighty-four per cent of the population live on 1.3 per cent of the land. In vast areas of Eastern Europe and the former communist world, depopulation is similarly acute. A 2005 census declared that 11,000 villages and 290 cities have disappeared from the map of the Russian Federation. Thirteen thousand villages remain, but with no inhabitants. Two villages, it's said, are 'disappearing' in Russia each day. I try to visualise them go, melting like sandcastles in the tide.[1]

I walked past a field where, too far away for a greeting, a man and a woman were turning the hay. Elsewhere, in the richness of the diminishing afternoon sunlight, there was a sheen on the waves of grass; the fields glistened, watery. The anthropologist Tim Ingold has coined the term 'taskscape' for that 'ensemble of tasks' that a landscape demands of those who work within it. In these fields, in the emptying valleys of Omaña, the taskscape has become frayed, and its acts appear to be ones that are more solitary than 'mutual[ly] interlocking': hay being turned or gathered, a net being spread over seedlings, some planting, the herding of a few cows.

And clearly we are prepared to give less and less to the taskscapes of Europe. In Italy, for example, where the birthrate of 1.2 is the lowest in Europe and where seventy per cent of farmers are over sixty years old, one third of Italian farmland is currently fallow. The implication of course is that the European landscape which so many love – the intensively cultivated, shaped landscape encapsulated by the German word *Kulturlandschaft* – is changing. Scrub is returning, the forests are reclaiming agricultural land. The continent's forest cover has expanded by almost ten per cent since 1990, and now Europe has

[1]'Perfect numbers like perfect men are very rare,' as Descartes said, and demographic data is of course variable – as are statistics for fatalities in war and numbers for immigration and emigration. The above statistics have been gathered and checked against a number of reliable sources, including the CIA World Fact Book and the Council of Europe's *Recent Demographic Developments in Europe*. Both of these sources are regularly updated. A recent volume on demographic trends, *The Power of Numbers – Why Europe Needs To Get Younger*, by Richard Ehrman, published by Policy Exchange in 2009, gives another slant on Europe's relative demographic decline: 'One hundred years ago, a quarter of the world's population was European, but by 2000 it was down to 12% and this relative decline is set to continue.'

more forest than at any time since the beginning of the industrial revolution. With the forests, packs of wolves have returned to the abandoned open-cast mining areas of eastern Germany, bears are back in Central Europe; in parts of France, wildcats and ospreys have re-established their territories; while, with human intervention, the world's most endangered feline species, the Iberian lynx, is beginning to gain a foothold in Andalucia.

This break with the long past is, in history's terms, startlingly recent. Even with mechanisation, harvest remained a communal activity up until the 1960s or even later. And, in the valleys of Omaña, as little as a hundred years ago, it is likely you would not be far from the taskscape that Ingold describes in his consideration of *The Harvesters* (1565) by Pieter Breugel the Elder:

> . . . you hear the swish of scythes against the cornstalks and the calls of the birds as they swoop low over the field in search of prey. Far off in the distance, wafted on the light wind, can be heard the sounds of people conversing and playing on a green, behind which, on the other side of the stream, lies a cluster of cottages.

¶

The road took a long sweep down into Villabandin. The village was held in a fold of hills, bright with broom. A silhouetted figure was walking towards me with a rolling gait, an uphill stride. She wore black: trousers and a top. I greeted her and she stopped, mildly curious.

'It's a fine day,' I said.

'Yes, it is,' she said.

'Do you live in Villabandin?'

She nodded and cast a backward glance at the village.

'Can I take your photograph?'

'Pah, no.'

'*Por favor.*'

'No. No. No. It'd break the camera.'

Her grey hair, like that of many of the older women in the region, was cropped short. She had faintly blue, milky eyes, but her nay-saying voice was strong, and her hands sliced the air as she refused my request.

'Oh, what a pity,' I said. 'I have come a long way to see Villabandin.'

'Well, there it is.'

'Yes, but I read about the village on the other side of the world – in Canada. A moment please.' I rifled through my backpack for the folded pages of the *Edmonton Journal*.

'Look.'

'Yes,' she said, pointing to the portrait photograph, 'that's me.'

'No!'

'Yes. Me.'

And I saw then that the photograph had caught her reluctance as much as her severity.

'Incredible!' I said and showed her the other photographs. She remained stoically unimpressed.

'*Buenas tardes, señor,*' and she continued up the steep, slow bend.

The cemetery, perched above the road on the outskirts of the village, was hardly bigger than a large living room. Its metal gate was unlocked. There was a row of white crosses and the family graves were set into the side wall, the names above them. Some were recent burials with inscriptions such as: 'Your wife will not forget you' or 'You are not forgotten.' The focus seemed to be less on remembrance than on a fear of forgetting, which, after all, is always more likely.

I entered the village, crossing the small bridge – one of two – from the Calle de Carretera. Above the town, the roofs lapped into each other, offering a show of unity to the fierce sun. But walking through its narrow lanes, the village disaggregated itself. So many buildings lay empty, and often the last act of abandonment was a symbolic resistance. There were planks held by stones against one door; a defensive mass of thorn branches, laced with broken glass, on the steps leading up to another. And where people hadn't erected barriers, nature had been complicit; tall, dark nettles shadowed the doorways. Coming from the gloom of one wooden door, slightly ajar, was the fusty, sweet smell of a barn as I remembered it from childhood.

Walking up one of the steep streets to the top of the village, I came across another old woman. '¿*Qué quiere?* she asked.

The implication was that someone coming here must have some specific aim in mind. Briefly, I told her my tale.

She had a round, smiling face, and she giggled when I said she had a beautiful smile. She was eighty-four, she told me, and had raised eight sons, all now away.

'Yes, it was hard work, but there was happiness. We were all together and there was not a bad one among us. Not one.'

A middle-aged man, a rarity, arrived on a small tractor, his wife following with a pitchfork. He had a handsome, devilish face with a broad, extravagant moustache.

'Yes, we are few,' he laughed.

We happy few: I was beginning to sense from the inhabitants of the village of Villabandin, much of it so close to being *abandonado y en ruinas*, that 'tragedy' was not a word they would use of their own plight; nor was it one that came to mind after meeting them. The article in the *Edmonton Journal* bore the subheading 'Slow, poignant end to a Spanish village'. Well, if this was the 'slow end', it seemed they faced their demise with equanimity. As far as I could tell, they blamed no one for the lack of work, the failed infrastructure, the lack of initiatives. They were inquisitive to know what someone might want of them; they were, on the whole, happy to be photographed. They made time to talk, but there was no sense of them wishing to prolong the conversation past its natural closure. No neediness. Of course, these might have been seasonal reactions. In winter, when the journalist came and when the village was whittled to its core, the answers may have been gloomier. For that journalist couldn't have said to them, as I could, '*Qué bonitos el paisaje, las flores, el campo . . .*'

The old woman pointed me to the school, close to the cemetery. I passed another redundancy: a collapsed basketball hoop rusting on the side of a wall.

The school was a solid, stuffy building, abutting onto the road. I peered through its windows, trying to take photographs of its interior: a few benches, a blackboard, the haphazard lumber that seemed to have no part there. There was a vacancy to the sunlight streaming in onto the desk. There is little more emblematic of a dying village anywhere than its closed school. A school, after all, is where the dynamic possibility of change is given focus and form. But once a school roll falls below seven in this region, its children have to journey through the valley to another school in a different *pueblo*.

When I turned away from the school, I saw an old man in a cap on a red chopper bicycle, the kind I associated with estates in the 1980s. He had stopped in the middle of the Calle de Carretera to chat to two young, tanned boys on mountain bikes who had come from the other direction. Their baseball caps had fresh, stiff peaks. The three of them were spread across the road. And why not? Not one car had passed in the last hour at least. I chatted to them for a while – the boys were from Malaga, on holiday staying with relations in the village; the man was a resident. I took a picture, then asked them to wait while I found the article on Villabandin. I was aware of their stillness and how it enlarged my fumblings through the backpack.

The old man exploded with delight. '*Ah, coño, coño,*' he said at the first picture. Then, when I opened up the spread, '*Coño, coño,*' again and again, as his finger jabbed at the familiar faces.

'I know,' I said. 'You see, Villabandin is famous in the whole world.'

The old man rose tall in his saddle. 'We live long here, you see. It is a good place for health. Pure air; tranquillity.'

But the young bikers confirmed to me there was nothing for them here. Though they smiled good-naturedly, I imagined they were grateful there was only a small part of the afternoon left to fill.

The old man on the chopper cycled off shakily and delightedly with his story. But others, like the ancient I'd met in the village of Montrondo two days before, had merely blinked at me bemusedly beneath his wide-brimmed straw hat. It had been as if the worlds we came from were already too far apart for the distance to be bridged.

¶

I returned to El Holandés Errante, the small hotel where I was staying in Murias de Paredes. I had serendipitously found my way to the hotel bar the day before, and Hans, the handsome, silver-haired Dutch owner, had asked if I was lost. No, I had told him, I most definitely wasn't, and I had showed him the newspaper article about Villabandin. He had shared his amazement with one of the regulars, and together they had identified most of the peoople in the photographs.

That evening, Hans was keen to know my reaction to Villabandin. As I was telling him about my meeting with the woman in black, his wife, Trina, joined us, bringing a plate of bread and *chorizo*. She had told me earlier that she had once worked throughout the community as a clown, but it was hard to believe that. Why would a woman so beautiful want to cover herself in face paints, to turn her natural grace into comic awkwardness? In the time I spent with her, I came to think it was part of her warmth, an expression of her generous nature; for, as she toured the small and shrinking schools of that region, telling stories, juggling coloured batons, she knew she was all the theatre the children would be likely to see. How great must their expectation have been, clinging to their small desks, lest excitement carry them skywards like balloons.

Trina and Hans made a handsome couple. They'd met on one of the popular islands off the coast of Africa towards the end of their previous marriages. 'His wife,' Trina confided in me, a glint of wickedness in her hazel eyes, 'oh, she was old and terribly ugly.' They had worked in boutiques next door to each other and still enjoyed relating the comedy of their revolving-door courting as they made up excuses to pop into each other's shops.

'The things you ran short of,' Trina said, 'the things you needed that you never needed before . . .'

Hans dipped his head and smiled.

Each had recognised early on in their relationship that, if it were to prosper, they would need to go somewhere new. The village of Murias de Paredes, where Hans had somewhat impetuously bought the grand old building that became their hotel, was familiar to them both – Trina had been there often as a child and she had taken Hans back there to share her memories of it. Her father had been a policeman in her home town and had been seconded to work as one of Franco's bodyguards when El Caudillo came to the region to fish and to shoot, obsessions for which he was renowned. The family came along with her father, and he and his wife liked the village so much they bought a house there and visited often, even when he was not on duty. Finally, it was where they had retired.

What had village life been like back when Trina had been a child?

'Oh, the village was full of life. But hard work – for the women especially. They had to work in the home, cooking and looking after the children. And they had to do agricultural work too, looking after the cows, milking and such. Each day they had to walk into the fields – and it could be a long way – and take lunch to the men.'

For what return? I wondered, remembering Lorca's lines in *The House of Bernarda Alba*: 'Two weeks in bed; then he moves to the table;/ three weeks later to the bar.'

Once, Murias had been the administrative centre of Omaña in Castile and León, but now it too was struggling for survival like so many of the villages in the region. Hans was an optimist, though, and believed it was possible to turn a village's life around. To him, tourism was the answer. 'The local people,' he told me, 'they are a mountain people; pessimism is part of their nature. Regarding depopulation, they are resigned to it. Unable to see that anything will come after them, they accept the fate of the village.' Hans and Trina told me of villages where one person lived, a herder; another where two brothers lived; another where –'Ah, no, that's uninhabited now.'

When Trina left, Hans poured another beer and we were joined by Chris Baldwin, a project-based English theatre director living with his Spanish wife in the population-poor edge of La Rioja. He was in his mid-forties with thick sandy hair, an affable smile and the comfortable look of a man accommodating a Spanish diet. His committed and dynamic work with the Spiral Theatre Company had grown out of an engagement with rural communities. I was keen to hear his insider knowledge of the emptying villages.

'Half a million women have left rural areas in Spain in the last five years.'

'Half a million?'

'Yes, but the point is that each woman represents a future presence of about fifteen people – some who may not yet be born. In other words, each woman's life is like an eco-system. Removing herself from the rural situation is like pulling the plug on a whole social network.'

He was in the region working on a project on forest fires. I think he must have seen my eyes glaze over, imagining predictable images of flaming matches and campfires with red crosses over them. But he told me how in the realm of rural depopulation everything became part indicator, part symbol, and that forest fires were no different. Farmers had always used fire as one of their tools. It cleared away old growth, the ashes of which fertilised the fresh shoots and revitalised the fields. The problem now was that an ageing and sparse workforce was unable to control the fires.

'For example, in 2005 in Galicia, just west of here, 45,000 acres of forest were destroyed by fire. And the last one around here spread across three mountainsides.'

'So, you write plays about the causes, do you?'

'No,' he said, 'that's not how I work. I would never parachute in a polished performance. I work to engage with community members about what matters to them, how they live in their world. In a safe environment, I create the conditions for people to bring up concerns that can then be discussed and dramatised. It's a long process and I don't set a time limit on it.'

It was a pity I hadn't arrived earlier, he said, or he would have invited me to accompany him to see the group at work in Riello. Riello wasn't much bigger than Murias de Paredes, but it had the advantage of having secured the school.

Chris told me that one of the exercises he had done with the group was first popularised by Augusto Boal, the renowned Brazilian theatre director and founder of the Theatre of the Oppressed. Chris had asked small groups to devise frozen images: the first one an *ideal* image of their village. What they'd most like it to be.

In the first group, two women cradled babies, made from folded jackets, in their arms. Another, on her knees, sucked her thumb, while holding the hand of the third 'mother'. The second group had imagined a wheelbarrow race. There was laughter when the women's skirts rose above their knees. The third showed children playing football.

'Ok,' Chris had told them. 'I'm getting very strong messages about your *ideal* villages. Now let's see what images you come up with for your *real* village.'

He gave them five minutes again, but they didn't need them. Nor did Chris need to go round each group. Four people in each corner sat on a row of seats, their shoulders hunched, their heads drooping, their eyes staring into space.

¶

The following day, when the workshops were over, although the project would last many months, Chris invited me to join the group for a celebratory lunch in the hotel at Murias de Paredes. It felt like the end of something; people were making one last attempt to forge a connection with each other that would survive their absence, draining the last sweetness from their shared experiences. For me, the meal also felt like the end of my first tentative understandings of how complex issues of depopulation can be.

The surprise, when I met them, was how many relatively young people there were – women with nose rings and plaited hair, bare-shouldered, their voices airy and light. They were students, home to their villages for the long summer vacation. They smiled their welcome at me. I sat next to Gabriela, an Argentinian woman. She was about thirty, loose-limbed, skin the colour of milky coffee and with high arching eyebrows over deep brown eyes. I imagine her beauty was why I talked to her most. Or perhaps it was because both of us were only there temporarily. She had decided to become a primary teacher, but wanted to do some travelling first, and had come to Spain. Over paella and *postres*, we discussed the week's experiences. Gabriela told me how good Chris was at his work, that he was a wonderful teacher, that it was amazing what he had achieved in one week working with them. But it had not been without difficulty. There were the inevitable conflicts that arise when people of different ages and different outlooks work cooperatively; these he handled with great sensitivity.

Gabriela said that many of the problems of the Spanish villages are shared by the rural communities of Argentina, although there the poverty is greater. Around the cities, shanty-town villages – *villas miseria* – cluster, while in the rural areas, 'There is no money to do anything.'

¶

I drove up the twisting mountain road that led to Valbueno. I parked beside the church with its out-of-kilter façade, its leaning bell tower offering commanding views over the village and towards Los Picos. Below it was the walled cemetery and a flat, grassy rise, where I sat on a rock to watch a vulture circling in the high sky.

Down in the village, I came across a woman sitting sewing. She wore the afternoon shadows like a cloak, appearing reluctant to look up from her work to talk. She had grown up here, she told me, but was only a summer visitor now. The young had all moved away; there was no one here but the old. And she bent her head again to her sewing.

I picked up a stick and strode out across the *altiplano* to Villadepan, passing through a landscape with rich gradations of green, brown and gold. The air was warm on the high pastures, the sky the purest blue, the sun on my face. On this occasion, isolation made my heart feel full. '*Maravilla volar, volar sin ver adónde*' (Wonderful to fly, to fly without seeing where), wrote Rafael Alberti in his *Second Chinese Notebook* about the elation of movement. Wonderful indeed to fly on such a day – or simply to walk.

I thought again of Laurie Lee and of the open road. In his essay about peasant tales in eighteenth-century France, Robert Darnton suggests that all such tales have two frameworks: on the one hand, the household and the village; on the other, the open road. The village was the place of security, of the known, of the mesh of obligations and satisfactions known as 'home'. The road was everything else – experience, escape, possibility, danger. Communities recognised its predictable pull, while mourning the losses it would bring. Hugh Brody tells in *Innishkillane*, his description of change and decline in the west of Ireland, how friends and family would gather in the parents' home to spend the night drinking, smoking, keening and playing games – 'the four most important parts of the secular rituals attending death' – before a son or a daughter took the open road, a road which would most likely lead to emigration. Brody tells of a rock called 'the Rock of the Weeping of Tears', where the accompanying mourners would take their last sight of the departed. But it could as easily be the top of a road, like the one my friend Mick pointed out to me in Sligo from the house where he still lived: 'And my uncle walked over that hill and his sister never saw him again.'

In *The Other*, a book of lectures about shifting identities in the modern world, Ryszard Kapuściński writes of the many people for whom 'the world outside is a source of anxiety, arousing fear of the unexpected, or even the terror of death. Every culture has a whole set of charms and magic spells designed to protect anyone setting off on the road, who is bid farewell amid outbursts of weeping and regret as if he were about to climb the scaffold'.

Kapuściński expresses here something of the tragic nature woven into what a Welsh speaker described to me as *hiraeth*. It is the feeling, she explained, of being drawn onto the road, beckoned to a place, but once you're there, to experience a heart-longing to be back. '*Hiraeth* is the thing that stops you from sleeping. It's the thing that wakes you up. But it is also the thing that is in your dreams.' It is, needless to say, one of the 'untranslatables'.

But it is not surprising that there should be a Gaelic equivalent – *ionndrainn*,[2] meaning that which is missing, longing: 'the old, throat-gripping wail', as Walter Perrie calls it in his poem 'Exilics: Leaving Lochboisdale, 1919'. Something of *hiraeth*, or *ionndrainn*, is at the heart of much discomfort associated with rural depopulation.

Ryszard Kapuściński recognises, in the psychology of rural depopulation, a thickening thread of unease across the globe, 'the result of a weakening of traditional cultural ties, caused by the migration of rural populations to the cities, where a new type of identity is starting to be formed – a hybrid one, previously unprecedented on such a scale'.

Throughout Europe – and across the world – many are drawn to vast cities, to find themselves kept awake by images of the world they have left. This Welsh folk song, the origins of which may go back to the tenth century, is unequivocal about the power of *hiraeth*. Here are its closing three verses:

The Irish Gaelic 'equivalent' is *eolchaire*, homesickness, melancholia, ennui. I'm told that in Galicia *morriña* carries the same meaning; in Portugal, *saudade*. Solitude makes a poem of iteration and echo.

In Another World: *Among Europe's Dying Villages*

Great *hiraeth*, cruel *hiraeth*
Hiraeth is breaking my heart
When I am sleeping at night
Hiraeth comes and wakes me from my dreams.

Hiraeth, *hiraeth*, go away, retreat
Don't press so heavily on me
Move a little across
So that I can sleep

The sun may pass, the moon may fade
The sea with its great waves
The wind as it blows strongly
But *hiraeth* will ever be in my heart.

Hiraeth cannot help but be nostalgic: with the passing of time, a particular place or person, rooted in a particular moment, can never be returned to. In this temporal sense, *hiraeth* is one of the great poetic tropes. For instance, it is something of the temporal aspect of 'Great *hiraeth*, cruel *hiraeth*' that Alastair Reid catches in his haunting poem 'The Tale the Hermit Told':

[. . .] I am sure of this –
that somewhere in my body there is a fiesta,
with ribboned dogs, balloons, and children dancing
in a lost village, that only I remember.

¶

There were voices in Villadepan, one of them the sing-song chatter of a child. Because of this, I knew they were not permanent residents. I soon came across a couple with their son. They were clearing some weeds from the front of one of the few houses not collapsing in on itself. The husband told me his uncle lived there, and, no, neither he nor his wife believed that people would return. I had arrived at one more of the many dead ends.

Yet, in the ruining village of Villadepan – and in all those others – the crumbling walls and shuttered windows were only the most obvious signs of abandonment. There was the intricate threading of all the paths that led into and out of the village – what Tim Ingold refers to as the 'meshwork' leading into the 'knot' of the village itself. Most of these were too slight, too 'informal' to be mapped, like snatches of a broken song. In neurological terms, if the villages were the synapses, then the paths were the nerves that once bore the messages between them. But not only messages – also story, anecdote, memory and purpose. The meshwork – the permeable lining I imagined at the start of my enquiry – was once the common mind of a locality. Which is why this family, playing at clearing weeds away, in the autumn motes of light, appeared somehow ethereal, momentary, freed from time; hovering slightly above the landscape – its secondary ghosts. Yet, although the stories that gave these paths their social meaning are lost, most of them will remain, as traces, as evidence for any people in the future who might need an indication of a route to take, where cultivation might begin again.

Here on the *altiplano*, I was reminded that other threads spinning out from the village would be the ones enabling the ancient practice of transhumance, the seasonal movement of people and livestock between pastures. On another occasion, I had followed one of these paths, climbing from the Auvergnat village of Dienne, high above the Vallée de la Santoire, to the Limon plateau. This had once been an important route for the Atlantic salt trade, as well as a site of transhumance. As the clouds grew blowsy, I had reached *la croix du gendarme*, erected in memory of someone who had perished crossing the plateau in bad weather. The cross had suffered here too; its horizontal limbs were no more. On it was Christ like a *poupée*, his large face atop a drawn-out beanbag of a body.

The plateau stretched like an undulating plain – its grasses had a parched, yellowy colour, dotted with hardy black hill cattle. It was easy to see how, up there, someone could have found himself lost if the snow began to fall; and, for this reason, *quirons* (cairns) had been laid at regular intervals to guide the traveller across the plateau and into the village of Veresmes.

As one memory folded another within it, I recalled following similar guiding stones – post stones – on a walk with my son to the dead village of Ceann Loch Reasort on Lewis. The practice of transhumance survived longer in Lewis than anywhere else in Scotland, allowing a sense of trans-geographical kinship with an older Europe. On the way, we had crawled inside a beehive shieling, one of the small stone huts where the herd would have spent the summer months. This is the first part of a poem I wrote about our walk:

One afternoon, we summered
in that stone womb, lips of light

whispering around us. We felt
the last of Old Winter's cold, smelled

the fervid stirrings of spring. Two bulbs
is what we were, squinting

at daylight and ready to push on.
It was fifteen minutes, no more,

that we squatted on the cool stones
and listened to the breathing of the beasts,

they already settled, the milk
gathering in their udders,

milk songs in the clear water
of the burn.
    But we had no other story

to tell, so we tunnelled out
of there and pressed on

dithering round a loch – pretty
but misplaced on our misread map.

A map, misread or not, may carry much of what is inscribed on the land, but the traces of individual memory – or of the imagination – it carries will have to be written into it. And who is to know how these stories will translate between an old man and his visiting grand nephew? The old, with their sticks and their broad-brimmed hats, staring at the incomers, those old people that Hans told me are resigned to their fate, could they be secreting somewhere a seed-bag of experiences and memories of a rooted life just waiting for fertile ground? Perhaps one seed has already been planted and this boy, play-helping in sunshine, might recall how a hoe is used with intent, how a scythe swings through the grass. There are times, among the lingering deaths of these villages, when, against all the evidence, it is necessary and restorative to remember that the future is not written.

¶

On my way back to Valbueno, I heard cow-bells, then a loud voice – a lone herder on his mobile phone, a voluble voice, as all voices in the rural silence tend to be. This was Alberto. He lived in Valbueno all year round, and for three months of the year was completely alone. Three or four other people joined him for the rest of the time. It got a bit boring, he told me, when I asked whether or not he liked the life, no one to talk to 'but the cows'. When I asked if I could take his photograph, he removed his straw hat and smoothed his hair. He was delighted to see the result. '*Un hombre de las montañas,*' I said. He agreed.

When he was a boy, there had been a school in Valbueno with nine or ten pupils, but everyone left – for the city, for abroad – and he remained. He waved his crook towards Los Altos Picos and told me how beautiful it was up there. There were silences in our conversation – unhurried pauses. He wore a pair of worn canvas *alpargatas* on his feet, and there was a paleness, like a salt mark, around his mouth. He must have been roughly forty, though a hard life is hard to gauge, and his blue t-shirt was stretched across his belly. I sensed his loneliness, but also his dignity and his courage. The last of his line.

In *The Farther Shore: A Natural History of Perception, 1798–1984*, Don Gifford maintains that, with the advent of modern technology, we all now live in an 'edgeless universe'. Nowadays, the Internet may well mean that the village offers possibilities for the skilled urban malcontent. It was clear, though, despite the fact that Alberto was using his mobile phone when I came across him, that his world had a very clear boundary, hard for him to cross and almost impossible for those who had left to re-enter.

What must it be like to bear that knowledge daily and to know that the dimensions of your life encompass you and the sixty or so cows you tend on the *altiplano*?

Driving back to the hotel, I found myself thinking about *The Yellow Rain*, written by Julio Llamazares, who was born in Vegamián, a small village in the region of León. The novella presents us with a first-person fictional account of the death of the village of Ainelle in the high Pyrenees through the voice of its last inhabitant. A note at the book's start tells us that the village was abandoned in 1970, that the village is actual, the characters invented. It is, by its nature, a work of vivid imagination, the site of the dead village being, as John Berger has expressed it, 'a site of no survivors'.

Llamazares' work is remarkable for the relentlessness and the intensity of its focus. The novella is an observational masterpiece of decay, through which memory stabs and haunts – the death through disease of the narrator's daughter, his estranged son's departure, the suicide of his wife, Sabina, whose instrument of death, a rope, he carries round his waist, as part tribute, part penance.

The narrator's dog is his only living concern, his ready comparison. He sees himself, 'forgotten by everyone, condemned to gnaw away at [his] memory and [his] bones like a mad dog that people are afraid to approach'. There is little that stands between the narrator and his death, and it is a tribute to the sensory qualities of Llamazares' prose that he retains the reader's interest – in short, isolated paragraphs – until the final denouement. It is from the start a story with a singular outcome, and yet, through it, Llamazares humanises the many villages with broken roofs and decayed floors, each of them a home, at some point, to the last in the line, an Alberto facing an inevitable future:

> . . . death has continued its slow, tenacious advance through the foundations and the interior beams of the house. Calmly. Unhurriedly. Pitilessly. In only four years, the ivy has buried the oven and the grainstore, and woodworm has entirely eaten away the beams supporting the porch and the shed. In only four years, the ivy and the woodworm have destroyed the work of a whole family, a whole century.

¶

In the village of Villanueva, a small, gap-toothed woman told me she had no intention of being here at the end. The people had all gone from her village because there was nothing there for them. The girls went and the boys followed, and for her, once she was very old or sick, the village would no longer be a possibility. '*No hay médico.*' Yet she remembered, like Alberto, that when she was a child, there had been many children at the school and village life had been very happy – fiestas, dancing with the accordion, all the people together. No, they wouldn't come back.

Still, I said, sometimes it only takes three or four families with children . . . She almost agreed, but then revised her opinion and concluded there was no hope.

She pointed down a path. 'Maybe thirteen people live there all year round.'

I followed the path down into another *barrio* of the village, where I came across Miguel, who I had met at the workshop celebration meal. He was sitting before his house, mending a scythe. No one had expected Miguel's redundancy so early. Though the nearby mines had been in steady decline, all had thought there were years of work left in them yet. The severance had been a good one, too good for him to seek other work without incurring losses to his package, although he was only in his late forties. He knew – who could not? – that his village was dying; it lay in a dip below the small main road and most people drove past without knowing it was there. Still, it was here that the family home stood, part of a row of houses with collapsing roofs and exposed beams. He was content in Villanueva the whole year; the *tranquilidad* suited him, he claimed. His two sons, both handsome with broad smiles, would of course leave one day to find work.

¶

Back at El Holandés, I ate and talked with Aryana, Hans and Trina's beautiful, dark-eyed daughter. We discussed her friend Celia and what she liked best at school. Religion. While we were chatting, a drink arrived for 'Braveheart' from a thickset, smiling man in his early forties. 'Hey, El Cid,' I called, '*Salud.*' Hans told me that Tino and his brother were down from Asturias for the weekend to shoot and that the bar regulars and they had planned a fiesta with me that night. Tino shouted that they were all going home to eat and would return dressed in their kilts. I laughed politely.

After midnight, I went downstairs to bid Hans goodnight. Tino was sitting on the corner stool by the door. I tried a goodnight. 'Hey, something to drink first – a night cap.' I agreed to a brandy, one of the good ones I'd had the night before . . .

How many did that lead to? I thought about eight, but Hans told me the next day that I all but drank the bottle. Before the brandy totally took hold, I initiated a discussion about *los pueblos*. Tino and his brother thought that there was nothing to be done. There was no work; they would die a natural death. I argued that if that is the case – and there was no other scenario they were open to – then there was a duty of care somewhere to manage the change.

I kept returning to Alberto. What would happen to Alberto? Is his life of work for nothing, simply to fill in the time: then he dies, his cows are taken elsewhere and his roof falls in?

'Ah,' said Hans, 'to you, Alberto is the key.' Yes, in some way, I believed he was.

Hans was guarded in this company, but earlier he had shown me an article that had appeared in the newspaper that day about the *sagaya* cattle, the most expensive meat on the market due to its low fat content. The cows looked like black bulls. Perhaps Alberto could herd these? Chris had talked of the end of agriculture as the mainstay of rural areas. What would replace it, as an activity around which community can be built, for him, was 'up for grabs'. He had suggested it could be a mixture of agriculture and tourism. Much seemed to rest on the increasing gentrification of the cities. With massive rises in house prices, house-owners could remortgage, buy a place in the country and therefore purchase what's produced there. Throughout Europe, some form of agriculture, supported by tourism, appears to be the most hopeful template, yet what was moving to me was the way that Hans and Trina had staked their savings and their energy in Murias in the belief that this area, for all its lack of infrastructure, would appeal to visitors. 'Build it and they will come,' was their credo. 'I am an optimist,' said Hans again simply.

But then, four brandies in, I was showing photos, my wife, my children, where I live, and then I was running, stumbling up the stairs, half-knowing I was gone, to get my Edirol recorder. I recorded as they pressed more drink on me. I recorded, as we toasted each other – layers of male voices close round a bar – and I recorded as they laughed and bantered with me. The clinking glasses sounded almost as if they would shatter. It was now singing time. They sang of their region:

> *Si nos preguntan*
> *De dónde somos*
> *Responderemos con elegância*
> *Somos de Omaña*
> *Somos de Omaña*
> *Bonita tierra*
> *De la montaña*[3]

[3]If they ask us/ Where we're from/ We will answer with style/ We are from Omaña/ We are from Omaña/ The beautiful land/ Of the mountains

And they sang of their village:

Viva Murias de Paredes
Viva el pueblo montañés.
Que si la villa muere,
España perdida es.

They were voices with drink taken, in other words louder than normal, but they were still strong and proud: 'Long live Murias de Paredes / Long live the mountain village. / Because if the village dies, / Spain is lost.'

In *Inishkillane*, Hugh Brody identifies the difference between winter drinking and summer drinking:

A drunken man in winter leans more heavily on the bar. He often seeks to draw another drinker or two to his side. Such a group creates a tight circle of privacy around itself – a privacy physically expressed by the arms they lay across one another's shoulders. Then, with faces almost touching, they appear to join closely in evident despair. This despair is not expressed in discussion among the drinkers. Rather, they exchange silence as if it were words, and words in brief expressions of the lonesomeness.

It is a drinking I have observed in rural Scotland. The grudging greeting; the disinterested silence. By contrast, of course, summer drinking welcomes the traveller and celebrates the place. It thrives on the incomer's appreciation of the beauty and tranquillity he encounters. It says, this is how we live here: open doors, lock-ins, impromptu ceilidhs, never a thought for tomorrow. What will you have? While winter drinking won't let you in, summer drinking is lethally congenial.

¿Estamos todos?
¿Estamos
Con las mujeres?
¿Amamos
Con los hombres?

Nos batimos
Cuando no nos conocíamos
Bebíamos
Y ahora que nos conocemos
Bebemos
Así pues
Bebamos

Bebió otro paladar
Y bebió nuestra madre
Borracha perdida era

El que bebe
Se emborracha
El que se emborracha
Duerme
El que duerme
No peca
El que no peca
Va al cielo
Así pues
¡Bebamos!
Hasta que no nos conozcamos[4]

[4]Are we all here?/ Are we/ With the women?/ Do we love / With the men?/ We fought them/ When we didn't know each other/ We drank/ And now we know each other/ Now we drink/ So let's drink// Take another swig/ Our mother drank/ She was a hopeless drunk// The person who drinks/ Gets drunk/ The person who gets drunk/ Sleeps/ The person who sleeps/ Commits no sin/ The person who doesn't sin/ Goes to Heaven/ So let's drink!/ Until we don't know each other anymore.

In Another World: *Among Europe's Dying Villages*

'Drink, until we don't know each other anymore,' ends this vigorous drinking chant. And in the bar, at the end of this outrageous bout of summer imbibing, Hans noticed, when I wrote, in my small recordings notebook, the date as '31 June', that I was a gone man.

I was outside of time, but not out of it enough to escape name games with Tino about Glasgow and Edinburgh rivalry. His toasts were always to Glasgow – our joint ones in praise of Asturias. The smoke was horrendous, a white chiffon hanging in the air and stinging my eyes. Tino offered me a Cuban cigar, which I refused. But I showed him a Cuban banknote, a souvenir I had carried in my wallet since a trip there some years before. There was much amusement at my magical production of it, and the men passed it between them. It was the time of night when even standing upright is a magical act. All the same, at one point, I forget now why, I was dancing. Alone.

¡Arriba, abajo, al centro y pa . . . dentro!
¡Arriba, abajo, al centro y pa . . . dentro!

Up, down, to the middle and . . . in!
Up, down, to the middle and . . . in!

But Tino declared, '*Estoy borracho,*' and he would not be persuaded to accept another gin and tonic. When they all left, the smoky bar was empty, apart from Hans and myself. I turned to Hans and gave him a victory salute. 'Amateurs! I saw them all off.'

'Yes you did. And it took until six in the morning.'

¶

That night, or what there was left of it, the brandy and memories of my conversation about forest fires with Chris combined to give me a troubled sleep.

I didn't know it at the time, but we were heading for an especially hot summer, with forest fires breaking out all over Europe – Greece, Bulgaria, Romania and in Spain itself. Such fires are not uncommon events around the Mediterranean, but that summer they were particularly widespread and severe. The Peloponnese was ravaged as the fires crossed arid land, where once pastures and orchards grew, and where there had once been people who had understood the ancient fire cycles and who had known how to harness their power. Fire storms surrounded entire, but depleted, villages. The desperate tried to save their houses, fighting the fires with garden hoses, buckets, branches. Several nights a week throughout August, as the fires reached their worst, we saw images on television of villagers' faces, drawn in terror at what they might lose, and the even gaunter faces of those whose homes had been completely eradicated. Many died – fighting or fleeing.

As I slept, those rapacious fires that would consume not only a vast acreage of pastoral Europe, but also large segments of our nightly news bulletins, lay two months or so into the future. Yet, after the cold and wet Scottish winter, the satisfyingly rich smell of warming, straw-like grasses was already beginning to permeate my dreams with a premonition of the scarred summer to come. As the summer I imagined heated up, my dream caught fire – a fire that spread across the mountainside from the neighbouring valley, so violent that it conflated in my dream with scenes from the Balkan wars: smoke pluming into the sky, narrow roads blocked with ageing refugees and their herds, cattle wide-eyed with terror. One cow slipped on the skitters of the others – I heard the crack of its hip and its bellowing. When its throat was slit, silencing it at last, blood poured across the narrow road, past the fountain at Lazado. There were no pretty hedgerows now, only the black charred limbs of trees, smouldering fields. After the walls of fire died down, the houses I saw – their fallen roofs, their smouldering beams – were little different from the ruined houses in any number of the villages I had recently visited.

¶

I woke at eleven and nursed myself through the day until three when Miguel and his sons came to take me on a drive around the local landscape. Hans had told him of the wild night and Miguel immediately said that if I didn't want to go it was no problem. But of course we went.

Miguel clearly had a lively intelligence, an enquiring mind and a nervous energy – displayed by his frustration when he couldn't get a point across to me. The car had bird books and plant books in its pockets. I sensed that, in some way, he was brushing up on the birds, flowers, lichens, insects, as if possessing the names of his world would give him some control over it and stop it slipping from him.

He taught me how to look at the landscape. Fifty or sixty years ago, he said, all the terraces were cultivated, *'centena y trigo'*. The word *trigo* triggered a memory of the island of Amantani on Lake Titicaca and an image of the terraces of the Andes. It transformed how I saw this landscape – no longer small villages in a natural landscape, but a landscape with a man-made presence everywhere and villages only concentrations of that presence.

Each village back then, Miguel told me, would have had eight to ten *molinas* (mills), small stone huts containing the mill wheel. Standing in the one on the road to Montrondo, just beyond Murias de Paredes, you can still hear the water rushing through. In the thirties and forties, his own village of Villanueva would have had ninety to one hundred children in it. Then each family had one to three cows. Now one person has forty to fifty. Improved methods of husbandry, but fewer people. The statistics are, of course, relentlessly expressive. Every village in those days had its own priest; now mass is said in each one in turn – once every fifteen days. But each church, even those in the most dilapidated villages, has a splendidly maintained roof. Is the upkeep of the tiny churches with their negligible congregations a statement from the Catholic Church that it will not abandon its flock? Are they – the survivors – regarded now as pillars, lodestars, strays or inconveniences?

I am not unaware – historically and personally – of the possibilities of change in rural areas. For seven years, we went on family holidays to a shore cottage near a farm outside Campbeltown in Argyll. Whenever I could, I worked on the farm, trying to pass myself off as a young farm-hand. The farm was a lively social centre, with its family, its hands and the holiday visitors. My parents found the damp in the cottage terrible, but for me being there was heaven – rounding up cows, dipping sheep; I even tried my hand at drowning two kittens. What I hated most was when the farmer's wife pointed me out as 'Tom – from Edinburgh'. I craved acceptance as one of them.

After my parents bought the cottage in the Highlands, I never went back to the farm until, just before we were married, Julie and I took a few days' holiday in Argyll. We were staying in a nearby village. Driving along one day, I glanced up the farm road. 'You should go,' she said.

The farm's air of desolation showed itself before we knocked on the main door. The barn doors were boarded up clumsily with crossed planks. Once, everything had been painted a serviceable battleship grey. Now all was worn and engrained with dirt.

Neil, the son of the former owners, was there, and he remembered me. He said that the heart had gone out of the farm when he'd had to sell the milk herd to pay his younger brother, a consultant, and his sister their share of the family inheritance. Shortly after the sale, milk quotas were introduced. This, he told me, with some bitterness, would have made the herd so much more valuable.

¶

Miguel took us up the twisting *camino de la montaña* to Salce and then up another valley to Curueno. It was stunning scenery, of course, but my stomach was churning and I was covered in sweat. He pointed on the map and said, 'Now we could go up there or over there,' his finger looping round another coloured gradient. 'It will take three or four hours.'

I had to decline. What great company, I insisted, but I wasn't feeling great. Last night. I couldn't escape a touch of shame, nor shield myself completely from his affable disappointment.

Back at El Holandés, I opened the bar door on my way up to my room. A few of the revellers from last night were sitting there. I mimicked panic and pretended to run. There was much laughter and enquiry after my health. I went upstairs to make a phone call and when I returned the bar was deserted apart from Hans, Trina and Aryana. I must have looked bemused. Hans told me they'd asked, 'Is Tom coming back?' When Hans said yes, they had all bolted from the bar.

That night I dreamt about the farm from my childhood. I was standing at the farmhouse door, but was aware of having to speak to Neil in Spanish, as that was his language now. I was trying to understand his story, as he, not a fluent speaker either, was trying to find the words to express it: a comment on the past, a foreign country, on how memory works. A sign, perhaps, of how difficult it could be, for these old people of the villages of Omaña, with all their lived stories, to access and to articulate the past.

¶

On my last evening at El Holandés Errante, I was the only guest, so Hans and I ate together. We discussed his plans to attract tourists to this isolated area with its depleted villages, and Trina served us rich chicken soup and mushroom omelettes. She claimed to hate cooking and said that two omelettes were *bastante*. She'd have something later.

Because it was late and because I was leaving the next day and so was thinking too much of myself and of how much I would miss their company, I never got round to asking whether Trina ever met the Generalíssimo herself or whether her father ever talked about what he was like. So I was left trying to piece together my own images of Franco, and of Trina's village youth, from what I had read of him and from what I had learned of her energy and playfulness.

What I would have wanted from Trina, I thought the next morning as I drove towards Astorga, the great red plain of Las Médulas spreading before me, the village already far behind, was the precious detail I could not get from anywhere else. Something revealing, of the kind Hemingway, in his early days as a journalist, caught of the posturing Mussolini in Lausanne in 1923:

As [the correspondents] entered the room, the Black Shirt Dictator did not look up from the book he was reading, so intense was his concentration [. . .] I tip-toed over behind him to see what the book was he was reading with such avid interest. It was a French–English dictionary – held upside down.

Franco, however, I felt sure, would be more guarded. He was never the comic opera figure Mussolini could be, nor even material for as inventive an actor as Chaplin. Yet, I had hopes that, perhaps, one day the unscripted moment might have arisen, like the one the photographer Robert Capa caught of Gary Cooper balancing his way across a tree bridge in Spain. Cooper holds a long fishing rod aloft in one hand and his stance is both precarious and balletic, his back foot turned inwards as he steps forward. But I realised Franco would never risk such a crossing, not because he lacked bravery; his courage was legendary: 'I have seen death walk by my side many times, but fortunately she did not know me.' The risk was rather in being unbalanced, in losing face. Even his conventional moustache took no chances.

Trina – the clown – could never be more different. I could see her in her youth, already beautiful, her body willowy, her face round and open, as her own daughter's now was, not yet possessing the Katherine Hepburn cheekbones that would eventually carry her beauty past middle age.

Possibly Trina's five brothers or one or two of the boys she grew up with were the first to share her sense of comedy – perhaps it was their laughter that fired her gift. Back then, they still ran and played together, her looks not yet something that set her apart. But even so, she had told me, when they became adolescents, little changed.

'Growing up with boys in the village, it is like brothers and sisters. You know each other too well for those sexy feelings to develop.'

I imagine it was this, as much as the sight of women working through all the hours of the day, that made her realise, back then, that village life was not for her.

59

The Village and the Road

2

I stopped briefly in Astorga, a small town that boasts a grand cathedral and a palace designed by Antonio Gaudi, now a museum. It is one of the main centres of population on the pilgrim route to Santiago de Compostela. The road out of it, the Camino de Santiago, is flanked by a scattered line of pilgrims with their staffs and small, clinking scallop shells. It is estimated that each year over 100,000 people make the pilgrimage. I was heading for the village of Rabanal del Camino to meet a priest with whom my good friend, Frank, a veteran of three journeys along the Camino, had put me in contact. I had seen a new or maintained roof on every tiny village church in Omaña, and was keen to speak to a priest who travels round the small *pueblos*. I wanted to find out more about the attitude of the Catholic Church – for certainly, in a village of collapsing houses, a new roof on a church is some kind of sign.

I had time to spare, so I veered off the Camino to the village of Rabanal el Viejo. Again, I found a place with that strange feeling of a village tumbling in on itself, yet with new buildings and renovation at its edges or, as often as not, between ruins.

I passed a goatherd who was whistling as she chased her goats out of their byre and onto the street. Their bells rang sweetly. One goat stretched its long black back above a doorway to sample some rose leaves from a fine display growing there. I turned to speak to the goatherd, and I saw her lock the wooden door with an iron key, the size of a man's hand, and then reach her hand into a cat's hole at the door's foot to hide the key.

'*Hola. Buenas tardes.*'

She was small, with smoothly matted grey hair down to her shoulders. Her complexion was nut-brown, and when she smiled she showed two sharp teeth – as white and gleaming as a cat's – on either side of her toothless gums. She wore a navy housecoat and brown stockings pulled up to her knees. She excused herself – she had work to do – and scuttled off through another wooden door into the muck of the yard, a whirl of energy and independence of spirit about her.

She could not have been more different from the international congregation of *peregrinos* with whom I attended evening vespers: clear neophytes in their responses to Gregorian chants. A group of schoolchildren had been shepherded to the front, and I enjoyed watching a boy carrying on a distant sign conversation with a friend. When he saw that I was observing him, he became serious and attentively spiritual. Afterwards, I waited around while the priest, Juan Antonio, dealt with the confessionals.

He ushered me into the monastery, into a small, dimly lit sitting room. There was an ease and an openness about him that soon made me forget the formality of his long, hooded habit. He had round glasses, short hair and a trim light brown beard, but he still seemed boyish. Widely read and culturally aware, his soft voice did not show the strength of his convictions as much as his hands did, framing his face as they rose to make a point.

Juan Antonio thought there was nothing to be done about rural depopulation. There had been enormous changes over the last fifty years in Spain; the social structures that had once supported rural life were no more. However, one must not forget that there had been enormous cultural changes over the past five hundred years too – during the course of which the 6 million inhabitants of Castile had dwindled to 2 million.

'Clearly,' he said, 'we are dying. And have been for a long time. For example, which route did you take to get here?'

'I went from Madrid to León.'

Well, he told me, I would have passed through Tordesillas. There, in 1494, the Spanish and the Portuguese kings divided the known world in the western hemisphere between them. Everything to the east of an agreed line of demarcation belonged to Portugal and everything to the west to Spain. Which is why, Juan Antonio explained, Brazilians speaks Portuguese.

'And just before Tordesillas, Medina del Campo – no, you won't have heard of it either – was once the New York of its time, the most important trading centre in Europe, selling wool to the Basque countries and beyond. Spain was, let us remember, once *the* world power. Now, we are a ruin of what we once were, though the cultural patrimony remains, one only matched in Italy and France within Europe.'

So, he wanted me to know, this was not the first time that great social change had taken place. And he advised me not to underestimate the poverty and the hardship of the life that had been left behind. He had once spoken to a man from a nearby village who cried at memories of the hardships he had suffered at six years of age. 'Then, you shared your house with a cow, a pig, a goat. Think of the smell. It was no romantic ideal.'

I asked him about the village churches with their new roofs. He told me what was obvious: that the (Catholic) Church was the only institution that still had a presence in the village. I asked whether he regarded the Church as a social service, given the withdrawal of all other support, owing to depopulation.

'For the Church,' he said, 'it is not a question of numbers, not of villages, buildings or social structures. Social structures change. For example, when I took my first pilgrimage in 1986, Rabanal del Camino was mostly a ruin. No, what concerns the Church is the person. The individual and bringing Jesus Christ into his life. Yes, for some, life might be hard, and those who are left – once the road has been built and everyone who can leave has left – are the ones without culture. They have no culture.' He said it emphatically, meaning their minds remained closed.

And yet, when Juan Antonio said 'culture', I don't think he meant the kind of image-conscious, fly-by-night culture that predominates now. Rather, he referred to a culture that is learned, inquisitive, aspiring. Spanish culture, he told me, had always been an aristocratic culture.

'Look at the touchstone, the most representative figure in Spanish culture – Don Quixote. He is a *hidalgo*, a minor aristocrat. And Goya, yes he painted village life, but also aristocratic life, the life of the ruling

In Another World: *Among Europe's Dying Villages*

classes.' And these, in Juan Antonio's view, constituted the significant art. I recalled the Goya cartoons I'd so recently become reacquainted with in the Prado. They were infused with the spirit of rural fiesta: a primary-colour vision of the completion of harvest, celebrated with dancing, singing, naughty-boyishness and flirting. It was the life of a clean earth – a beautiful abstraction of the reality.

But Juan Antonio also emphasised that it was a question of quality of life. 'Here, I have time. Time to read, to reflect, to listen to music.'

And perhaps, I thought, for these 'culture-less' villages, the satisfactions are equally basic – a tranquil, predictable life, with the solitude to recall their lives and to put them in some kind of order – and, if they're lucky, with children nearby to visit them.

Yet, still, at the end of my conversation, during which he had been open, stimulating, helpful, I was touched by some lingering sadness. Those few villagers clinging on were condemned – and aware of their fading future – for innocently letting history dismantle them, for being ignorant of high culture, for their own helplessness. Juan Antonio's recognition of what would pass – though not immediately and not in all villages, as the case of Rabanal attests – was without compunction. His faith meant that village survival wasn't his prime concern: rather, he was focused on the human individual and the individual's soul.

One of the ironies of speaking about depopulation with Juan Antonio was that above the entrance to his monastery, so recently founded, was the legend in Latin:

Sancti estis deicit dominus
et multiplicabo numerum
vestrum ut oretis pro populo
meo in loco isto

You are holy, says the Lord,
and I will multiply your numbers
so you will pray for my people
in this place.

¶

Back in León, I had a meeting with Rosa, an *animadora comunitaria* whom I had met briefly in Omaña. We walked to the library, talking about the villages. She was open, intelligent and patient. Yes, she understood my difficulty in getting the villagers to talk. They lacked confidence, and, with so few people around, they were out of the habit of speaking to people. She rejected the idea of the rural population of this region being without culture. They *were* cultured: they had songs and ancient traditions. The ones who were left in the villages – the ones Juan Antonio had said were without culture – were rather those whose minds were not open to the possibilities of change or those who had family responsibilities. As for the church roofs, Rosa agreed that the church was the only institution that had not abandoned the villages, but the beautiful roofs were mainly paid for by ex-villagers themselves. It was very important to them that the church roof be maintained.

Rosa had already spoken to the librarian, so when we arrived there were neat paper markers in the pages of the various volumes of the *Diccionario Geográfico, Estadístico, Histórico, Biográfico, Postal, Municipal, Militar, Marítimo y Eclesiástico* DE ESPAÑA *y sus posesiones de ultramar.* Bookmarked and photocopied for me were entries from 1868 of the villages I had visited – Murias de Paredes, Villabandin, Villanueva. In a short uniform paragraph, the salient features of each village were listed. I noted how each was tied into a religious, military and political bureaucracy, yet I also saw how little of exception they had to offer – small parochial churches which received the most inexperienced priests, the monoculture of agriculture, buildings which lacked anything of note. Each village unremarkable – '*Nada de notable.*'

During our discussions in Murias de Paredes, Chris had told me how unattractive the villages continued to be to teachers. Roughly half of Spain's children go to private schools: it is the most extensively privately educated group in Europe. Spanish teachers are reluctant to work with composite classes in rural areas. Student teachers must choose a region and sit public exams, *oposiciones*, designed to counter their ambition. The student teacher is then put somewhere on one of the *listas*, a grading system. Those who are low down on the list, or who have failed, teach at schools in the rural areas. But only for one year; then they try to move on. It could be that a teacher posted to a school in a village may be a middle-class woman who picks her way with high heels through the dirt. The feeling that everything is below her must transfer to her pupils. This problem, Chris has told me, like so many of the problems affecting depopulation, is one of mentality.

¶

Over *tapas* of quails' eggs and a glass of Rioja in one of León's lively bars, I talked with Rosa and her partner, Chema, an educational psychologist. We discussed the state of mind that must be invoked knowing you are the last of a kind. Again, I thought of Alberto. When Alberto goes, a way of life, a whole perspective on the world, goes with him. Yes, Chema agreed, and he cited a village he knew where the youngest was seventy years old. '*La más joven!*' But these people, he said, were narrow in their outlook and very religious. They believed in suffering and in paradise – whatever happened to them was an act of God. Yet in fact, the earthly reasons for depopulation are often remarkably clear.

Alastair Reid, whose childhood in Whithorn in southwest Scotland has given him a life-long affinity with villages, observed what happened in Deya in Majorca, where he once had a house. He remembered how the charcoal burners would go down into the valley, and, at the end of their day's work, would each return with a 'column of charcoal as high as a man' on their backs. The village collapsed as a centre of self-sustaining work when bottled gas began to arrive at the ports.

'It killed the charcoal-burning overnight,' he told me. The men had to go down to the coast for work, and that began the slow erosion of the village as a self-contained way of life. And then the tourists began to arrive. Alastair has a telling anecdote about how they affected the village economy.

'The mayor used to run a barter system on market day. Villagers would arrive with their produce – hens, vegetables or whatever – and be given a chit that allowed them to trade for the other produce. It worked remarkably well. And then the first tourists arrived and all they had to offer was money. The village economy was killed off quickly.'

To George Lovell, Professor of Human Geography at Kingston University in Canada, a fractured sense of community can lead to a village's demise. This might happen, for example, if the village school is closed down. In 'The Solitude of Solanell', he describes what happened in the Pyrenean village of Solanell when its school closed and the children had to travel elsewhere. The result was that 'two hours of potential labour was lost in their travelling back and forth' or – in even worse cases –

> children were boarded, cutting them off from their families for most of the week. The effects of this removal meant systematic socialization to ways other than those of parents and grandparents. In school, bonds were formed and interests sparked that might later lead to marriage with a non-local partner or employment far from home. Towns like Solanell thus gradually became abodes of old people, places where the younger folk were conspicuously few. The manner in which children were schooled in essence educated them to leave. Towns without children are destined to die [. . .] are half-dead already.

Yet there was still a way of managing change; of valuing the lives and the experience and the culture of the villagers that remain. It is what Rosa did. She had recorded their songs and, when I met her, was interested in their lullabies. But she told me there was little interest from the government and no funding to do such projects. Her work as *animadora comunitaria* wasn't simply that of an extra-mural provider of activities and courses. Rather, Rosa had to respond to what the people themselves wanted.

'But the old want nothing,' she said, sadly. 'In times of hunger in the 1920s and '30s, they'd known people who had to walk to the cities – Barcelona and Madrid – to find work in order to keep their families alive. Then came the Civil War, which affected them all. Then forty years of Franco. Now there is this economic boom, this new prosperity, but their minds are already channelled – they just want to sit in their houses and watch television.'

In terms of cultural activity, Rosa found, they only wanted to talk about their lives, but Rosa's boss was not in favour of this.

Rosa worked not only in Omaña, but also in the Riello district, where there were forty villages and just a thousand inhabitants, making it the most scattered population in Europe. In all of La Luna, she told me, there were no more than sixty children. Rare things.

Chema used to work informally, visiting the villages, as there was 'much depression'. In one village, they had found an old mill, and, once it was restored and was working again, it became the focus of village life. People would gather around it and begin to speak to each other again, to tell stories till two in the morning. The habit of conversation among so few, for whom so little happens, falters. I recalled how, back in Murias de Paredes, when I had had some difficulty with a plug to charge my camera, it had become a group project, its resolution greeted with an excitement that seemed more than simply the pleasure of helping a stranger. They were 'animated' by it.[5]

Still, Chema said, even where the Spanish economy was burgeoning – in the confident major cities to where the rural exodus head – there was great poverty. He had recently read that in the suburbs of Madrid people were surviving on one dollar a day. Madrid is one of the places that Canadian writer Doug Saunders terms an 'Arrival City', a place to which rural people come because of previous connections there. Using this existing network, they set about improving themselves and their opportunities, supporting their families through education and social welfare. The population shift to the cities will, he feels, lead to a control of population in the developing world.

[5]The document *Regions 2020, Demographic Challenges for European Regions* (2008) states clearly that the 'Implications of rural change [. . .] will depend on participation rates, particularly for the elderly. "Human capital" is the guiding principle of sustainable economic development.' It is also, as Chema points out, essential for the social mental health of those who remain in rural areas.

And what of those who remain in the villages? Those who are too old or too limited to cross the threshold of the village boundary and embark on the road to the city? Those who remain surrounded by the crumbling buildings and the fields where they have spent their lives, waiting to be swept into the 'dustbin of history'?

69

The Village and the Road

3

I first met Marian – Maria Angeles Huarte de Davidson – over thirty years ago. She had left Barcelona to marry Jack, who was, at that time, working as a solicitor in Dumfries. Marian was born and grew up in the village of Funes in Navarra. Although, for many years now, the couple has lived in Edinburgh, she and Jack return to 'the village' every summer, as they also did while their two daughters were growing up. Her experience has given her both an insider's viewpoint – her father had once been mayor of the village – but also a more detached perspective on village life and the changes she has seen. It was serendipitous that, during my trip to Spain as I worked on this book, she was taking a summer course in Spanish literature at the University of Salamanca, where she was once a student.

Marian's affection for Salamanca was clear: its grand university buildings, its colonnades and its magnificent cathedrals. Like many thousands before her, she had once stood before the façade of the ancient university and sought out the hidden sculpture of a tiny frog. Legend had it that its discovery, among all the forms that writhed there, was a promise that she would find love within the year. She laughed as she told me this, but gave little away.

'Today,' she said, 'students throw the remains of ice-cream cones at the relief of El Caudillo.' It is one of the medallion portraits of 'great men' that run around the rim of Plaza Mayor. Sometime soon the authorities will tire of cleaning paint-spatters from it and remove it, this symbol of old fettered Spain. Not that there aren't things worth holding onto as well.

'Long live Death!' the fascists had shouted at the university during the Civil War. 'Death to the intelligentsia!' But it had not deterred the Basque philosopher, Miguel de Unamuno, the ageing rector of the university. Addressing the nationalist audience, which included Franco's wife and the belligerent General Milan-Astray, Unamuno had answered:

> This is the temple of the intellect and I am its high priest. It is you who profane its sacred precincts. You will win, because you have more than enough brute force. But you will not convince. For to persuade, you would need what you lack: reason and right in your struggle.

The speech had cost Unamuno his life. Hounded out of the university, he had died of a heart attack a week later. Both love and death were in the legacy Marian inherited as a graduate of this ancient place of learning.

But, for all Salamanca's nurturing, Marian felt most closely attached to her village. 'The village is part of Spain's identity. Everyone comes from a village sometime. The village is my roots, my country.' Not that this fact has made her any less aware of the shortcomings and realities of village life. They are the obvious ones of people taking too keen an interest in what one is doing, a preconceived view of where one should go in life – preferably, somewhere within the village.

'All the feelings of the universe are there,' she said, her voice light with an insider's affection. 'Love and hatred and, in times of crisis, support.'

But her village, like every village, was marked by the Civil War. Everyone knew everyone else, and it was that intimacy, rather than any strong political beliefs, that made the war so painful.

'The village was very divided – the very rich and the very poor. Like the whole of Spain, from north to south. One, two or three families owned most of the land. Some saw the Civil War as the opportunity for them to own land. Of course, that was not possible after the Civil War. Then the divisions became even more obvious.

'People lived in fear during the war. Some families were very badly affected by the experience. My family didn't like to talk about it. For example, in some villages, they shaved the women's hair and paraded them through the village. My mother was appalled by that. And the people involved were not especially politically minded. For them, it was mostly an occasion for revenge. There was one woman I know to whom it happened. She was very attractive, but she had no strong political ideals at all. I can say that, because I know her still. It is likely that it was jealousy – or a desire for revenge – that brought her before the kangaroo court.'

El pacto del olvido – the pragmatic decision to let the past lie – was broken in Funes in the late seventies and early eighties. It was the families' decision to dig up the bodies of those who had suffered summary execution. Marian was no longer living in the village at the time and her recollection of events was vague.

'All of sudden somebody knew where the bodies had been buried. Yes, it was regarded as a good thing. Although, there was one man who did not want to know where his father was buried. This was frowned upon.'

These disinterments took place many years before the Law of Historical Memory was passed in 2007. This entitles anyone to be given assistance in excavating a mass grave if they can provide evidence for its existence. But about whether the exhumations led to resolution, Marian was unsure. Perhaps, in her absence, there had been some coming to terms with the past, or perhaps, equally likely, forgetting became a habit that was hard to break and harder to share.

When Marian left for school, and then for university, it never crossed her mind that staying in the village was an option. Yet the village can still surprise her. When her mother died, she was buoyed by the support she received. She had always been concerned how she would react to the traditional viewing of the body, but in the event people were wonderful and allayed much of her fear of death. She recalls one woman who brought grapes to the wake, remembering that her mother had liked them. 'A poor woman,' Marian says, 'somehow she got grapes for my mother.'

There has always been work in her village, and now it has attracted a sizeable population of North Africans, so that the village is split into the old one, where most of the long-time residents live, and the new one across the river to where the younger population has moved. There is not racial tension at the moment, rather a simple division in terms of race, religion and language. Such an influx is one of the possibilities for the dying villages of Spain – the return of 'the Moor', upon whose banishment, ironically, much of Spanish identity once used to rest.[6]

But however these changes affect the character of her village, Marian told me she would always return – and her daughters too: it was part of who she is. 'Wherever you go,' she said, 'you make a social network. In the city, you can make a kind of village too. But even if you create a *barrio* in the city, that *barrio* will be made out of concrete, not out of *la tierra* – earth.'

[6] *Regions 2020* gives some background to the demographic shifts affecting Marian's village of Funes. It tells us that Europe's immediate neighbour, the Middle East and North Africa region (MENA) has the world's fastest growing population after sub-Saharan Africa. (For example, the population growth in Turkey is projected to reach twenty-three per cent by 2025 due to its young age structure and its high birth rates.) One in every three people in the MENA region is aged between ten and twenty-four. However, the MENA region also exhibits the world's highest unemployment rates – over twenty per cent of young people and over thirty per cent of young women were unemployed in 2005.

The Village and the Road

In Another World: *Among Europe's Dying Villages*

Neighbours

Juan sits in the shade of the pines and looks across the valley and the *altiplano* to the high peaks. Beyond them lie Asturias and the sea. The mountains are violet, insubstantial as the air that surrounds them. Even as a young man, climbing over their highest passes, he'd had to stop to lean on his thighs, drawing in oxygen with great looping breaths.

He has woken early, foregone breakfast and instead come here with a bowl of milky coffee to calm himself while he waits. He would have gone to Luis himself, but the years have caught up with him and these days he has to massage each leg, pounding it with his fist merely to stir it into action. So he waits, imagining Luis complaining about the walk to see him. Luis – at fifty! Huh, at fifty, Juan could have walked all day, crossing every valley till he came to the capital. Sometimes, for work, he'd had to, sleeping out under the cold stars, and all without a word of complaint.

He can picture Luis coming, with his small man's big strides, his arms swinging loosely by his sides, his contemplative expression as he thinks about yesterday, or tomorrow, but never the present moment. He'll have climbed the twisting road from the dip in the valley where his village lies, close to the river, rolling his broad shoulders, a light breeze at his back. The small oaks will be waving to him as he passes. Will he be noting the small finches in the hedgerows? The snow-burst of wild white roses? The tell-tale blood of a poppy on the verge? Juan thinks Luis ought to be alive to all these small pleasures. Now that the life of the earth will soon be lost to them both, each should raise his eyes to the air, to the faint pinks of blossom, to the winged yellow chest of a finch, flitting from slight branch to slight branch. Juan has seen bigger candle flames.

But no, Luis' mind will probably be, as ever, elsewhere, studying nothing beyond the patch of road where each foot falls. Juan fixes his gaze on a buzzard high above him, circling in the warming air. It has been years since he has been able to read a newspaper without screwing up his eyes, but his far-sightedness has never left him.

In a couple of months, summer will be here. Already wild roses make the hedgerows precious, the forgotten gardens and pastureland are overgrown with clouds of cow parsley, purple daubs of foxglove and vetch. But in high summer, the hills will flame gold with broom. By then, the summer residents will have arrived, flush with their city stories, keen to work on their houses, to refresh the ideas they hold about themselves – mainly that, although they have travelled far, they are rooted in this earth: at heart, they are still villagers.

Why are there more of them in Luis' village than in Juan's? Why the luck of blood that means Luis' village, among its ruins, has a handful of whitewashed houses with neat winter shutters and slated roofs? After all, the names of their villages share the same root; both carry the river's name. Yet it seems to Juan – and who could deny it? – that his village has borne more deeply the ravages of abandonment. Little else but collapsed walls, broken beams, rooms given over to the beasts. Still, sitting in the vaulted silence, on this rocky spur with its views across the valley, he cannot even begin to imagine living anywhere else.

'Views,' Luis once grumbled. 'Hmmph. You can't eat views.'

Or perhaps Juan's wife had said that. Certainly it sounds like one of the comments she liked to throw at him, the kind of thing she said more and more often until she told him she couldn't face one more winter here and, just like that, left for the city with their three children – Juanita, Manuel and little Leo. In their absence, they have remained children to him – he sees them hiding behind the pine trees, throwing stones at birds, although they're all grown up now. Why don't they come to see him? Other children do, drifting over from Luis' village with its pretty houses and flowering pot plants. They circle him shyly, if their paths cross, and Juan feels he has become overgrown and unkempt and hides his awkwardness in silence.

Why is it, he wonders, that the church is kept locked nowadays? Juan feels a sudden urge to come face to face with the blue-clad Madonna once more. He thinks of her with longing and fear. Would there be understanding or judgment in her eyes? Strange, this stirring of the old faith that had abandoned him long ago. Not suddenly, as his wife had, but like the village, drifting away bit by bit, until he was left one morning staring into a blue he recognised as all there was of life.

At one time he would have thought, who would take a few candles? Who would make firewood from the chairs where people had sat in prayer, no matter how terrible a winter might become? But now, nothing was certain. And his faith, he sees now, had been part of that clear, fierce world his father had come from and out of which his father spoke.

In the long winter months, when the road verges were like small cliff-faces of snow and they were alone in their villages, Luis and Juan had sat late before a dying fire and talked of their fathers. Juan felt almost scared when the subject came up. He feared that, from nowhere, his father might surprise him from behind Luis' chair. 'What's this you're saying about me? You dare to talk about how distant I was, how harshly you think you were treated?'

They can see, so clearly, their own fathers' failings, yet neither Juan nor Luis have fared well as fathers themselves. The evidence is painfully obvious. That pair, it is said throughout the valley, like their own solitude, happy as pigs in shit.

Juan's father never let him forget that his son's birthday was the date that marked the end of the Civil War. It was either some kind of sour honour or it was reason to lose one date in the obliteration of the other. Since his father's death, Juan had kept his birthday a secret, folded away in shame like his father's pistol that was kept tucked inside an old blanket in the attic.

But this is *New* Spain. Even in the mountains they are told it. And what does that mean? Nothing for Juan and Luis. Abandonment. Loneliness. Houses falling into themselves everywhere they look. Thank goodness for old friends, Luis said, once a snowstorm surprised them and he'd had to overnight with Juan. Juan agreed, saying nothing, but nodding and letting the warmth wash through him as much as he could allow. For there was something impersonal about the way Luis said it, as if it were just one more of the proverbs which gave shape to their lives.

And Juan knows Luis can be devilishly selfish. Put simply, Juan's good fortune became Luis', but it rarely happened the other way around. Once, for example, Juan came into some tins of beans that arrived over the mountains from Asturias. 'Here, take these,' he said to Luis, lifting at least half a dozen of them from their shallow box. And he wanted no objection. Yet, when Luis had a good crop of potatoes the year Juan's were blighted, nothing came his way. How can a man ignore such things, pretend they have never been?

When they go to the bar at the crossroads, down at the foot of the valley, Juan likes to think he's not the only one who notices Luis' arrogant manner. He sees the way the others look at the small man who hammers his glass on the wooden table when he's making his points. 'At least with Franco . . .' His lip begins to tremble and Juan shakes his head with the others: 'Pah. Pah. Pah.' Luis glares round the table, the smiling faces, his hand tightening round his glass.

Juan pummels his sleeping thighs, turns onto his hands and knees, and slowly gets to his feet. An imprint of himself remains in the moss and pine litter. He takes his bowl back inside the house. In the bedroom, a slick of sunlight dapples the chest of drawers. In the dimness, the light seems as tangible as one of the lace cloths his mother loved so much to make – something delicate in this raw world.

He fits his fists to the round handles and the drawer slowly jerks open. He parts the old grey papers from his carefully folded suit, momentarily finding it strange that the pinstripe still runs through the brown cloth after all this time. The shirt and tie he won't bother with, but he feels the suit is fitting. It connects him to the important events of his life: his wedding, his children's christenings, the funerals of his mother and father. Then they were a village. And, when they were a village, there would have been a dance on a few of these occasions – an accordion in the street, bottles passed around.

He buttons the jacket and looks in the webbed mirror.

Of course, he isn't expecting to see youth there, but he is surprised to see such an old man, the set of his mouth reminding him of his father as he lay in his coffin on the table where the white bowl now sits. Another old man in an ancient suit.

In Another World: *Among Europe's Dying Villages*

Luis must know as well as he that *la tierra* is all they have left. And that it means the same to them both. Luis had only to ask. If only he had. But to move the boundary sticks, without a word, to increase his own grazing! Only then had Juan noticed the richness of the section of ground he had stolen.

At first, Juan thought it had been in error, but there was no talking to Luis. This was his ground, he claimed. He had found the old maps that would confirm it. Was this 'New Spain' too? And had Luis signed up to it? What would Juan's father have said about such a 'New Spain'? His father's own brother had been shot for just such a disagreement. His name had been written on a scrap of paper and passed to the authorities. It was common back then. They bound him up, his father said, his voice cracking. 'I'll only tell this story the one time.' He hadn't seen it done, just watched, through a slit in the window, a flock of sparrows rise suddenly and fall back to the earth, into the dust in which they had been bathing.

'Come. Let's talk.'

'Nothing to say.'

'Come anyway.'

'If you want. But I tell you, I won't change my mind.'

Luis will be across the straight now and coming round the slow bend; the village will be before him. The road horseshoes around it, then begins its steep, twisting descent to the valley below, where it meets the main road. Juan feels a sudden burning shame. So many of the huddled roofs of the houses are like fish-bones, the turf falling in. Hedgerows, like burst mattresses, spill into the small fields around the village, shrinking them further. And Luis, looking up at last, might be smiling to himself. No, fuck Luis! Juan feels his own shame, his life's shame, as Luis walks towards his village.

¶

The gun had looked strange, and at first he'd left it lying on the old blanket. Both blanket and gun had a fusty, metallic smell. Then his hand reached out and he took it up – one hand to begin with, then the other to steady it. He felt a boy again, a boy in his father's eyes.

He won't sit on the earth again, for fear of dirtying his suit. He has shrunk into his jacket and its tails reach down to the backs of his thighs. He sits on a stone bench instead, feeling the chill now he's out of the sun. There's another ruin at his back. The Merino family had lived there. Destroyed by drink, his mother used to say of Señor Merino. 'And once he was the pick of all the *guapos.*' Sometimes, a light and secretive smile could flare on his mother's face. He imagines he hears the Merinos bickering over a pot of stew, the children like birds around their slumped father. 'Look at you now, my beauty,' Señora Merino is saying. 'Look at you, you great lump of uselessness. Oh, that I fell for your tragic eyes!' She raises a fist to box his ears and Juan feels the children rush past him, heading towards the open fields and the cities beyond.

A handful of the cows that companionably shared the shade of the pines with him pass by. Their hooves rattle on the broken tarmac, the light polishes their brown coats to a sheen. A couple of them stop on their slow progress to the trickling fountain and look on him with indifference. His beautiful beasts.

He hears a car.

Luis – lazy, good for nothing Luis – hasn't walked at all. He'll park his car at the entry to the village, slam that troublesome door he's never got round to fixing, curse it if it doesn't close.

It's almost midday, so Luis leaves very little shadow on the road; nor does Juan when he heaves himself up and steps out to face him. By Luis' own admission, there's nothing to say that has not been said.

¶

The bullet lodged to the side of Luis' spine, so he will be able to walk again. But those who told me this story, late one night at the bar at the crossroads – after, I confess, so many brandies that I may have some of the facts wrong – say that Juan is the lucky one. A gun that hadn't been fired in forty years! It could as easily have blown up in his face.

When they took Juan away, he never told them why he'd done it, shrugged whenever they asked, 'Isn't Luis your friend?' He just took the porridge they offered him and felt a blank fill his mind when he tried to speak.

Then he asked, 'Who will look after my cows now?'

The Lesson

She remembers the schoolroom,
   her desk third from the front.
She could still draw a plan of it –
   who sat where – still sees the plait
of Luisa's hair before her. No matter
   how tightly it was bound,
rogue hairs caught the light,

distracting her from whatever
   the teacher was saying. Today,
something about how,
   in comparison with farmers,
hunter-gatherers had a much easier life.
   So why settle? They thought
of their fathers, up at dawn,

working the dry earth, coaxing
   the green shoots that would one day
bear fruit. But not without
   an endless watering and worrying.
And they thought of their mothers,
   pressing their faces against the great swell
of the cow's belly, working the teat

as milk drilled into the pail.
   As for them, they had duties too.
But, at heart, weren't they the true
   hunter-gatherers? Each summer
on high pastures, filling their skirts
   with berries, the boys finicking
with their traps. Yet each year

came with sterner warnings
    of the farming life that waited
to draw them in. So, eagerly,
    they waited for the answer:
'Though the hunter-gatherer
    moves freely, the farmer stays
to beautify his residence and to keep guard

over the dead. Even elephants,'
    the teacher tells them, 'tend the bones
of their dead.' When Luisa lay
    in her coffin, the same plait, though white,
wound round her head. It was November,
    snow thick on the ground; spring
before she was able to put a posy

on the grave. She has seen all
    the hunter-gatherers depart
and now she farms the dead.
    But after she's gone, who will tend
her grave? Who will whisper her name,
    as she had once her own true friend's,
in their schoolroom at the day's end?

Stars

When he was young and powerless,
    he liked to put his hand over an eye
and lop the ends off the village –
    first one side, then the other –
as his mother topped and tailed carrots.

Sometimes, he would divide
    the village by taking out the church
or, better than anything, the school.
    He revelled in vacancy, in making
his own bit of night. The shock

was in the possibility of there being
    a different village when he'd grown
into this one, learning its complex
    geometry of intimacy, such that
there was little difference

between his life and the life
    of the village: when he thought of one,
the other instantly came to mind.
    So rooted was his world in the village
he once dreamed stars were buried

above its roofs. They surfaced
    like vegetables – turnip moons
hanging each night from the darkness.
    Strange then to find himself
driving through another darkness,

his lights disappearing like water
    into the dry earth. His village
lies behind the next black curve,
    but built now of something so fragile
he could lay it on the palm of his hand,

scatter it among all the rotting shaws.

PART TWO

Lost Lands

—

The Lost Land

Sunlight through leaves,
*   stippling bands*
across a road
*   just before it curves*

It's possible to love
*   when love*
is a fixed point,
*   going nowhere*

The French historian Fernand Braudel has taught us to examine the present for what survives in it of the past: a felt boot, a proverb, a snatch of song, a ritual linked to the land. In other words, the threshold between the past and the present is porous.

In the world of the dying village, everything becomes an image of loss: an abandoned jar, a broken chair, a rusted bridle-bit, a felt boot, a proverb spoken out of context, a snatch of song, a wooden switch, the villagers themselves. Memory takes us by the hand, crosses the threshold into a lost land. A lost land, but one that we can visit from time to time, and one that visits us.

¶

The road to the village of Laurie, in the high Auvergne, passed through a landscape of rolling, wooded hills. The banks and hedgerows were overgrown and unkempt. Cow parsley and thistles, their silvery down wandering gently downwind, leaned into the narrow road. The spiked heads of teasel marshalled themselves against thickly twining

In Another World: *Among Europe's Dying Villages*

brambles and dark-massed nettles. Some fields were unfenced and apparently without purpose, others had extravagant loops of slack wire marking their boundaries. Tumbledown stone walls meandered patchily along the hillsides like Morse code, evidence of terrace farming long since abandoned.

I parked a few hundred yards from the village at the head of the valley. The only sounds were of a cockerel clearing its throat and a distant cowbell. The silence was immense. Before I gave myself to it, I was aware of a tension created by the stillness, the lack of movement. Something impending.

Early in my travels, I had decided to record segments of what I had thought of as silence – at the time I'd imagined there would be a quality to silence, some aural evidence of the thinness of life. I played one of these recordings to Sara Maitland, author of *A Book of Silence*. For a number of years, Sara has been a student of silence, following it until she arrived at one of its sources in the Galloway hills. And the silence she listened to as she walked through the settlement of Laggangairn, abandoned during the Lowland clearances, was as complex as any sensory experience can be:

> This beautiful wild silence exists under the shadow of the people silenced in order to create it. The silence of oppression, the silence that does 'wait to be broken' and needs to be broken in the name of freedom, exists inextricably tangled with the *jouissance*, the bliss of solitude [. . .] The price of this silence is silence. And it suddenly felt very expensive.

One of the conclusions in her account of her journey is that there is no silence this side of the grave; our own heartbeat conspires against us. So the silences I returned with inevitably always have inverted commas around them – they are, at best, notated silences.

The two minutes of silence that I played to Sara had been recorded in northern Spain, on the edge of a small village. She commented quickly that it was a common rural 'silence' – cowbells, birds, a river flowing, the odd bark, a distant lowing. Of course, these are the sounds we commonly associate with 'silence' of a rural nature, but there are also soundscapes of greater complexity that can elude us. These are the evanescent sound environments of rural human activities that fade away as depopulation of the countryside occurs.[7]

On mainland Europe, the most dominant village sound was once that of the church bell. The towers still stand in many villages, though the villages and the bells are largely silent – or, as in one French village I passed through, a tape of ringing bells is played on a loop. There is such nobility in the curves of a bell, whether housed in its tower or framed by a blue sky in a gable end. In *Village Bells: Sound and Meaning in the Nineteenth-century French Countryside*, Alain Corbin explores the importance of the bell in French life. It announced events of significance and defined territory. On 2 August 1914, when general mobilisation was declared in the countryside, the peasants assembled beneath the urgent peals of village bells, and it was said that President Mitterand owed his 1981 election victory to a poster showing him standing at the foot of a village bell. Given all the resonant meanings of the bell in French life, it is understandable that its silence carries equal weight. Corbin writes:

> The bell was regarded as a support for collective memory and with good reason. The people long preserved the imprint of its sonority [. . .] One cannot help but be struck [. . .] by the existence of a long memory that is particularly attentive to the silence of the bells, a phenomenon associated with defeat, humiliation, sacrifice, plague and interdict.

[7]The project *Touring Exhibition of Sound Environments* (TESE) set out in 2000 to record the sounds of Harris and Lewis in order to preserve the individual elements of the soundscape, in the same way that one would safeguard any other natural or ethnographic material from falling into oblivion. Among the forty-six 'tracks' are recordings of 'vibrating strap and bolt on old trailer', 'electric wool washing machine', 'cockerel and croft ambience', 'A. D. Munroe's [Tarbert] Mobile Shop arriving at MacLennan's' and 'CalMac old ferry and public safety announcement'.

For it would be a mistake to assume that silence is either passive or neutral. The imagination, whether from its acquaintance with history or from its sensitivity to environment or circumstance, also hears the absences – or the presences – within the silence.

¶

I passed the small *auberge*. A handwritten sign on the door said it had closed for the day at quarter past four in the afternoon. One sharp curve above it, I found the heart of the village: the tiny boxlike *mairie*, the war memorial, the church, the cross, all jostling around a square the size of a tennis court.

The damp, dark church was open. It sucked in the sunlight when I opened its door, then breathed it out again, leaving me in crepuscular light. I could have used a candle's flame, but all the spikes for that purpose were bare. The church had its full complement of statuary, though: Christ crucified, the Virgin Mary, a minor saint or two – all glowing dimly or drawing shadows around themselves.

Out on the square again, I listened to the steady overflow from a stone trough, noted a wooden switch someone had left there. Apart from the fall of water and the occasional bark of a dog, this was the kind of silence that draws you to observe the growth of vegetables – the fullness of cabbages, the thick, creamy limbs of leeks.

There was no one walking out of the houses with their geranium flourishes, their open shutters, to take a stroll along the road. There was no one sitting in the shade, no sign of the companionship of a Spanish village. A tractor passed. I waved, and the driver mouthed a silent '*Bonjour*'. I returned to my car and, past Laurie, continued to twist and turn deeper yet into the silence, up the narrow road towards the tiny hamlet of Lussaud, a thousand metres above sea level on the plain of a volcanic landscape.

¶

'The road has the air of never deciding where the country it's heading for lies, at the foot of the forests, in the high pastures or on the edge of the plateaus,' Pierre Jourde writes in *Pays Perdu*, the book that had brought me to Lussaud. In the novel, Jourde draws on his experiences of the time he spent on holiday as a child and an adult in his father's birthplace, as well as on the privileged knowledge he had as one of the village's intimates. In this 'Outer Mongolia', among gods called 'Alcohol, Winter, Shit and Solitude', stories are revealed of adultery, disability and death.

Pays Perdu is framed by a winter journey the narrator makes for his father's funeral. This device enables him to reflect on experiences of the village, its inhabitants and its secrets, including a clandestine affair. Jourde controls two narratives, the first concerning the funeral – its arrangements, the burial, the wake. This is conveyed with great clarity. The second narrative concerns the revisiting of childhood. It's from the tension between these two that the novel gains its power. Because, of course, the 'lost land' refers as much to the narrator's childhood as it does to the village he revisits. For land is never lost from those who live there; it is only lost to those of us who cannot get back to the world we fully inhabited as children.[8]

'Have I ever been there, this lost land?' Jourde's narrator writes. 'I lose it, I don't stop losing it.' And yet, the paradox is that this 'lost land' remains, for the narrator, unchangingly there.

Parisian literary critics compared the novel to *Le Grand Meaulnes* and saw it as a fascinating revelation of *la France profonde*. Not so the inhabitants of Lussaud, who, once the substance of the work had filtered through to them – the book was stocked in a village some kilometres away – reacted with anger and hurt. Jourde, aware of mounting discontent, sent letters to all the villagers, saying that he

---

[8]This is the force of the French *pays*, which Graham Robb defines in *The Discovery of France*: 'The word *pays* – usually translated as "country" – referred not to the abstract nation, but to the tangible, ancestral region that people thought of as their home. A *pays* was the area in which everything was familiar: the sound of the human voice, the orchestra of birds and insects, the choreography of winds and the mysterious configurations of trees, rocks and magic wells.'

In Another World: *Among Europe's Dying Villages*

had changed names and dates and telling them, 'You mustn't look to it for an exact representation [. . .] I'm proud to be from Lussaud.'

Jourde's next visit to Lussaud was in July 2005, at the start of his summer break from his university lecturing post in Grenoble. Six villagers arrived outside his house and began shouting insults. Stones were thrown, then punches. His children were called 'dirty Arabs'. Jourde and his family fled.

Three women and two men, one of them the seventy-two-year-old who had discovered, through the novel, that he was the progeny of an adulterous affair between neighbours, were given two-month suspended jail terms and fined. Should Jourde have been surprised? He had taken care to disguise names and dates, but he must have realised that public interest, knowing his background, would look on the novel as a *roman à clef.*

He seems to have thought that it was acceptable for him to appropriate stories, as long as he screened the outside world from the exact people involved. But the residents of Lussaud clearly took exception, not simply to the newsworthy revelations, but also to the depiction of their lives. The legal representatives put it succinctly. While the magistrate stated, 'All Pierre Jourde has done is to describe the solitude, the pain, the promiscuity,' the villagers' defence lawyer told the novelist: 'You write about their lives and their vices, you do not look for what makes them tick. You manipulated them. You played with them.' This strikes me as an overly severe judgment on Jourde, who describes with great sensitivity the harshness of many of their lives, from Lulu, a girl with learning disabilities to Joseph, the celibate, and Felix, who had spent his adolescence 'lying in the stable with the beasts'.

The loneliness of the landscape – 'You can walk all day, under the full sky, without seeing anyone, but herds of red cows and horses' – and the isolation and repetition of routine make alcohol a welcome companion, but one that blights existence:

Alcohol entered into the blood, it bred there, it broke up the family, you could see traces of it in the faces of children. It prescribed destinies, you conformed to its imperatives, with fatalism, without taking pleasure from it, nor really forgetting.

The placidity of life in the novel is underscored by a hidden violence, accidents resulting from alcoholic errors; but, in spite of these human dramas, the changeless nature of village life weaves through *Pays Perdu*: 'In these old mountains, everything, like the work of the peasant, repeats itself unwearyingly.'

Jourde could be said to be giving voice to a distaste for rural life that is deeply rooted in French metropolitan culture, a distaste that exists despite the city-dwellers' respect for the gastronomic delights that originate from *les provinces*. In *Peasants into Frenchmen*, Eugen Weber describes the disgust felt in eighteenth-century France for the physical and mental world of the peasant, 'the savage instincts born of isolation and misery'. Manuals of etiquette were sold by pedlars advising how not to walk like a peasant or eat like a peasant. And Weber writes that, well into the nineteenth century, 'village midwives kneaded babies' skulls in an effort to give the little round heads of peasant babies the elongated skull associated with intelligent city folk'.[9]

Nonetheless, the reception of *Pays Perdu* was not unusual. It was, for example, a fate that had earlier befallen Chekhov's short story, 'Peasants' (1897). In Chekhov's case, censors objected to the 'too black a picture it

---

[9]Frequently, throughout history, the terms 'peasant' and 'villager' have been synonymous. Both have shared certain economic circumstances. Eric Wolf, in *Peasants*, points out that one of the defining features of peasants is that they are 'rural cultivators whose surpluses are transferred to a dominant group of rulers', while Clive Aslet, in *Villages of Britain*, describes villages in terms of their obligations to their lords: such villages, 'put roofs over the heads of the families who toiled on the lord's fields and kept his sheep, managed his woods or dug his mines'. Though 'peasant', in the sense of a dependent subsistence farmer, is one that progress in the West has supposedly made redundant (and Weber in the quotation above is clearly using it to refer to a particular historical period), it is still the term resolutely favoured by John Berger to frame the last members of a particular socio-economic group, and it also has a continued relevance in the developing world (for example the Via Campesina movement). However, for the purposes of this book, I have used the term 'villagers' and hope that, when I have introduced the word 'peasant', the context makes clear why I have done so.

In Another World: *Among Europe's Dying Villages*

paints of peasant life'. In fact, it has much in common with *Pays Perdu* in its descriptions of drunkenness – 'Our men are a lousy lot of drunkards, they don't bring their money home!' – and its sensory distaste for peasant life – 'The tea was revolting, just like the conversation; which was always about illness and how they had no money.'

Writing about rural life is problematic: the danger is to write sentimentally, as, for instance, Lorca can do, or anthropologically. Positioning and distance, but also respect and empathy, become crucial considerations. Seamus Heaney – one of a number of writers whose concerns touch on such a theme – announced his dilemma and its solution in his famous early poem 'Digging', in which he resolves to dig not with a spade, but with a pen.

There was a barking of dogs and I broke off a switch from a fallen tree beside the cemetery. The walled cemetery was fifty yards or so from where the village started, on a small rise overlooking the valley. It was reverently well kept. Even the older family tombs had flowers in them, and many had racks of those durable messages about endless love and promises of remembrance, 'the habitual formulas', as Jourde describes them:

> And the Christs agonise, these candles weep, these eternal regrets exhale without end, among the absent-minded mountains, in an absolute silence, broken sometimes by a quick agitation of beasts, at the foot of the bushy surroundings.

Lussaud was a cluster of stone houses and farm buildings. Some buildings were in excellent repair, and I wondered which one Jourde was keeping vacant. The handful of streets and lanes led me to a cube-shaped church with a spire. In *Pays Perdu*, I remembered, Jourde describes the villagers within its shadow version mumbling through hymns they didn't know the words of.

An old man studied me from his garden and bid me a '*Salut*'. By the church, I met a hearty woman, stocky and strong, just past middle age. I told her how pretty the village was, and the lie that I'd been lucky to chance upon it.

'You like it?' she asked with an edge of suspicion.

'Yes, it's charming. Very tranquil.'

'Oh, tranquil, yes.'

'And, in winter, do you get much snow?'

She looked at me now as if I was slightly imbecilic.

'Of course. We are at one thousand metres. Lots of snow.'

'So you are cut off?'

'Yes, we are cut off.'

'Is it hard living here, then?'

'No, I've lived here all my life. It's not hard.'

'But not many young people now, eh?'

'Ah, we have enough young people.'

Just then a van arrived and Lussaud's one senior pupil got out; she was bespectacled, blonde, wearing a sweatshirt. The woman took her backpack from her.

'Oh, heavy,' she said admiringly, though I could only think that the weight of learning the older woman now admired was probably what would carry the girl from the village for good.

¶

I loitered at the mouth of the village, by a broken and bleached wooden cart. There was a burst of evening activity – a string of cows processing towards me, a bull with two calves. The herds were being brought in by three tiny dogs and two old bent women.

I was experiencing what I had felt at Valbueno, high on the *altiplano* in the Omaña, after standing with Alberto watching his caramel-coated cows take to their new pasture – a reluctance to leave. It can't be coincidental that both Valbueno and Lussaud are mountain villages, often cut off by snow. The fields here were rich and well kept, dotted, like chessboards, with black stacks of silage. I heard cowbells, shouts in the distance. There was the sense of being close to – of feeling the reverberation of – a natural rhythm, born of necessity. Such is the pastoral feeling Andrzej Stasiuk elegises in *Fado*, his book of essays about village life in the Carpathians:

> [. . .] what about the animality that's embedded so deeply in our lives? What about the cattle that live so close to humans? What about the herds of cows returning at dusk from their pastures, lifting their tails and shitting in the middle of the village? What about the cattle smell, which reminds us where we really came from? When that disappears, when it vanishes from our everyday existence, there'll be nothing left that is capable of assuaging our loneliness.

Far from the great agri-plains of northern France and central Spain, the resonances of village life echo from culture to culture and through time and literature. The elements are strikingly similar: a group of people and their stock and their livelihood on the land. Everywhere, the push and pull factors of village life. Yes, the community of the village, but the restrictions the community puts upon you. Yes, the prospect of security, but the claustrophobia of predictability. Yes, the attraction of a life lived through the rhythms of the seasons and in proximity to animals, but also the tyranny of nature from which much of human endeavour has tried to free us.

In its huddle of stone buildings, it is easy to see the claustrophobia that could have engendered Jourde's fictional version of Lussaud and propositioned its dark possibilities to him. If you were to look for signs, you might find them in a suspicious glance, in a set of boar's hooves nailed to a door. But on the other hand, there was the well-tended graveyard, the ostentation of flower-boxes, that slow, cooperative rhythm. Whatever dark sides Jourde brought to his tale, he must have been hoping that they would be balanced by the glimpses of intimacy, friendship and love that the village also harboured.

In Another World: *Among Europe's Dying Villages*

Of Armoires and Wolves

Each night, its kindness
made the village glow

Wolves patrolled its roads,
letting no one
either in or out

The cathedral of Saint-Pierre stands at the sharp end of the great basalt rock on which Saint-Flour, a town in the south of the Auvergne, is built. I gazed up at its dark towers, made of the same volcanic rock as the cathedral in Clermont-Ferrand, which was described by the writer Vita Sackville-West as being the 'blue-grey of a pigeon's wing'. The building had a certain gravity, one which made me feel sombre rather than uplifted. Standing in the Place d'Armes, where the narrow roads of the town converged, I turned to look out over the valley below, which, that morning, had held a nest of thick fog.

The regional Musée de la Haute-Auvergne was next to the cathedral in the former bishop's palace. I visited close to the day's end, wandering the spacious rooms alone, in muted but golden sunlight. There were displays of furniture, unusual instruments and traditional clothing from the region. Ornate eighteenth-century travelling chests, which suggest the limitations of ownership and the instability of life, gave way to a great hall where the massive farmhouse armoires from the following century hulked against the walls.

The owners of these heavy, nearly immoveable pieces of furniture were people whose being was the polar opposite to that of the nomad. The great armoires did not convince with finesse, but with character. Seven feet tall, with a dark burnish of time, their doors had latches like those on the sturdiest of gates. Their decoration was similarly unfussy, with large square or diamond-shaped panels.

'Does there exist a single dreamer of words who does not respond to the word "wardrobe"?' wrote Gaston Bachelard in *The Poetics of Space*. But times have moved on, since the publication of Bachelard's book in 1958, and it seems we are no longer willing or able to build the faithful relationships with our furniture that we once did.

I recently phoned an auction house to enquire about two chairs we wanted to sell. The auctioneer came round to have a look at them.

'Worthless,' he said with a glance. 'One's part of a three-piece Edwardian suite. The other would be illegal for me to sell. Fire risk.'

'Then what should we do with them?' I asked.

'Dump them. They're worthless.'

'But isn't there some charity that would take them?'

'Look, you couldn't give them away.'

'Really?' I was shocked.

'Lots of people bring me stuff and call on me to look over their possessions. Often they're older people from a generation that was used to looking after things. Make do and mend kind of thing. And what they want is permission. They want me to say it's okay for them to dump their stuff.'

'They're good chairs,' I insisted, wondering whether he saw me as part of an 'older generation'.

'I'm sure they are, but no one wants them. Problem is that the bottom's fallen out of the student market. That's where a lot of that stuff used to end up. Now they just get a starter pack from IKEA. Costs them £300.' He delivered all his gloom in a brightly positive manner, knowing it was enlightening me. 'Put it this way, I've got someone starting with me today, full-time. After one week, he'll have the equivalent of a degree in psychology. He'll know what's important to people, what they can let go of and what they can't.'

'We've got a nice grandfather clock,' I said to him as he left.

'Yes, I noticed that.'

After he'd gone, I slumped into the Edwardian armchair and felt laughter rising in me until it turned into guffaws so deep I had to hold my hand to my pulsing heart. Worthless! It turns out that most of what we all have is worthless. Yet we spend so much of our lifetimes marshalling it, maintaining it, until the next generation is called upon to get rid of it, shelving not only our own past, but whatever shared memories they have of it.

It felt at the time like the most precious and absolute piece of wisdom had triggered my laughter. But later that week, destroying a small wardrobe in my daughter's room – it was, after all, worthless – I was ambushed by the companion piece of wisdom, expressed by the novelist Oscar V. de L. Milosz, that 'A wardrobe is filled with the mute tumult of memories.' As I took a hammer to the joints of my daughter's wardrobe and pulled the sides apart, as cleanly as filleting a fish, I saw, hanging in my mind's eye, the small, embroidered dresses that had once hung there.

The darkness that fills an IKEA cabinet or small wardrobe is a slight thing, its flimsy wood exposed in the compressions of end-pieces, the roughness of boreholes. Your piece of furniture does not arrive over-bearing, brooding with the mysterious darkness of a forest at its heart. Whereas it is not hard to imagine the behemoth of a French armoire in a farmhouse kitchen, the firelight shining dimly on its chestnut door, allowing in just enough light when opened for a hand to reach for what it wanted. But not enough light to illuminate the sides, two dark pillars where anything might swell out of the darkness.

When I was a child, in a world where darkness was more common than it is now, I was terrified of a piece of marquetry, little bigger than a fist, which topped off our grandfather clock, the very one to which the auctioneer had given such cursory notice. It is in fact a floral decoration, a plant growing in a small pot, but I saw in its figuration a bearded face. Of course, there is something primordial about our tendency, particularly when we're young, to see a face in anything and everything: candle wax, clouds, curtain patterns. The tiny head controlling the mummy-shaped bulk of its clock-body made me think of an all-consuming grub. Its small face was angry-looking, somewhat oriental, and therefore – it was the fifties – more terrifying. And no matter how much it disturbed me, *because* it disturbed me, I could not un-see it. That small but threatening presence in the hall could not become again the tame plant it had once been.

¶

Wandering through the hall of armoires in Saint-Flour, I imagined a child who sits by the fire, watching how the light plays on the surface of the armoire, a great beast casting shadows as it reveals its shape-changing nature. The boy knows this enormous mass has adopted its form only temporarily; it could at any time break from the mould it has been given, and reform itself into whatever terror a mind could create. For was it not born in the forest where fear grows like leaves?

Sometimes at night, he hears the oak stretch and creak, as if in discomfort. He knows it is not at home here among domestic objects: plates, knives, linen. No, the armoire has brought something of the forest in with it. The silence of its depths, the shadows between its trees and the trees that become shadows. And it has brought in something of the forest's temptations as well as its fears. And these too are secret. Just as I never told anyone how I had feared the animus of the grandfather clock as I raced down or upstairs past it, alone, so this child also recognises that his fears are both real and a product of his imagination and that through the armoire he will be testing a darkness in himself, a darkness he is frightened he will not be able to control.

I imagined what he smells: the earth, the firewood burning, the tallow candle, the oxen's breath, the smell of the women – sharp, lingering, mysterious; he almost tastes it on his tongue. It is evening, of course, winter, and people have gathered for a *veillée*, an evening of work, talk and song.[10] He is with the women, close to the light of the fire, as they sew and mend, narrowing their eyes for the delicate work, their fingers quick, their faces glowing, animated as they talk, telling stories and swapping proverbs that encapsulate peasant experience and wisdom:

---

[10]The equivalent in León is a *filandón*, a word derived from the Latin *filum*, or thread. Like the *veillée* and the ceilidh, this was a night when the women sat spinning while everyone told stories.

In Another World: *Among Europe's Dying Villages*

When we have nothing left, we will have nothing to lose.
To get his hands on the money, a man will marry a bear.
Don't fart higher than your arse.

Beyond them, as the light edges into a grainy darkness, the men are engaged in work that their hands have the sight for: they sharpen and clean tools, they check the efficiency of their traps. They crack walnuts in their fists.

The child, sorting vegetables, is glad they are there, shielding the armoire from him. Through its doors, the forest, the wolves. How close has he been to a wolf that has been alive and not hanging, teeth bared in a dying rictus, from a tree? He has seen its broad head, its thick brush, its coal-dust spattered back. But has he seen how its black lips have a half-smile? Or how its amber eyes are wild, eyes that say, with no room for doubt, *We need to kill together to stay together.*

There was, according to Gillian Tindall, the author of *Célestine: Voices from a French Village*, something pathological in the pursuit of wolves in the French province of Berry throughout the nineteenth century, something irrational that had its roots in tales of werewolves. There was a price on each wolf's head, and they were relentlessly hunted.

A small corrective to their extermination is now to be found in a park about sixty kilometres south of Saint-Flour, where wolves are bred and kept in semi-captivity. From a walkway, I looked down on one of the spacious wolf-runs. There was a wolf on the path in the sunlight. I imagined myself there, as a traveller, facing it. My heart raced, our eyes briefly locked, then there was that uninterest wild things have for us and he padded off into the brush. While such close-ish encounters are designed to actively neutralise the worst calumnies against the nature of the wolf, the attraction, named Les Loups du Gévaudan, still trades on the horror story of the Bête du Gévaudan, which terrorised the area between 1764 and 1767, purportedly killing twenty-five women, sixty-eight children and six men. In *Monsters of the Gévaudan: The Making of a Beast*, Jay M. Smith tells us that by 1765 the beast was one of the most famous living things in Europe and argues that it was the narrative transformation of the wolf pack into a single monster that accounted for its particular terror. However, there is still doubt whether it was a wolf or a psychopath that was responsible for the killings – it is said that in some cases young girls were undressed before being devoured.

At the visitor centre of the park, I browsed the history and picture books telling the tale of how two huge wolves were killed – each possibly the *bête*. Over the years, illustrators had created a gallery of the beasts. Some drooled through pointed teeth; others were upright, with muscular thighs and broad manly shoulders. These images seemed to encapsulate Eugen Weber's concept of 'peasant neurasthenia', an anxiety fuelled by fear: 'Fear of the night, of thieves, of neighbours, of the dead. Of menaces known and unknown – above all wolves, mad dogs and fires . . . they were always afraid of something.'

In the *veillée*, a story is being told – the one about a wolf encountered on the forest path. Common wisdom has taught the boy that it is better not to come across anyone by chance on a path, never mind a wolf! The wolf weaves its way into the darkness. And, as it does so, the boy, testing his mettle, must be the one to go to the armoire to fetch a blanket. He must train himself not to snatch or to pull and so to bring a pile of carefully folded garments and blankets spilling into the room. And, if he fails, he must learn also to keep silent as his mother berates his stupidity. After all, how can she know what lurks on each shelf, waiting to clamp itself round his hand? She will be even less aware of how the armoire calls to him to step through its door, not into a world of fantasy adventure, but into a real forest where the wolves, with their sharp teeth, their silent paws and their yellowish night-vision eyes, hold every advantage. There, he will either be eaten or learn how to become a man.

The belief that Gillian Tindall identifies in *Célestine* of 'the world behind', the mysteries beneath the surface of life, is one that could easily be understood, in any time, by any child with a vivid imagination. More so in a place, where as Robert Darnton writes, 'the sound of the baying of wolves gives a touch of realism, not fancy' to a story. Such a place was the Auvergne in the middle of the twentieth century, where, for many, Weber's words 'they were always afraid of something' became horribly apt again.

¶

By all surviving accounts, Oradour-sur-Glane had been a spirited and welcoming village in the years leading up to 1944. It enjoyed a varied social life, being within a tram ride of the city of Limoges. It was a popular destination for day-trippers, who came to fish, visit the fair or while away time in one of its many cafés. It had also welcomed refugees from the Spanish Civil War and was now sitting out the closing scenes of the Second World War with quiet intent.

To visit the Oradour whose life was ended on 10 June 1944, you have to walk through the Centre de la Mémoire and up the steps to the 'Village Martyr'. A small booklet, *Oradour-sur-Glane: The Tragedy Hour by Hour*, written with admirable clarity and restraint by Robert Hébras, one of the survivors of the executions at *la grange Laudy* (Laudy's barn), creates something of the chilling events of the day on which 642 people were massacred, beginning at the moment when the armoured vehicles cut off the village's arteries and its inhabitants were commanded to assemble at the fairground.

At first they had thought it was only an exercise to inspect their papers. The mood darkened when the men were separated from the women and children. The men were to be massacred in small groups at different locations around the village. Hébras surmises that he himself survived only because the German forces couldn't be bothered moving their machine guns further back. As a result, most of the men were hit on the legs, not the upper body. However, this condemned many of the survivors of the shooting to an abominable death through burning, for, after the machine-gunning, the soldiers covered the prone bodies with hay and firewood and set fire to it.

The massacre of the women and children, held all together in the church, began when the first shots of the executions were heard. From that inferno, only one woman, Madame Rouffanche, escaped, after having seen her closest relations die around her; the SS, irritated by the continued cries of those asphyxiating from the noxious smoke in the church, began to fire through the windows of the sacristy: 'Beside me, my daughter, the youngest, was killed by bullets which cut her carotid artery.'

Of Armoires and Wolves

Hébras describes what it was like for the first people to enter the martyred village:

> Every step was unbearable agony, so numerous and abominable were their atrocious discoveries. The stench of burned flesh hung over the ruins, still groaning in pain. Here were two entwined bodies, which seemed to have been spared by the flames, though they crumbled to dust at a touch; there, two children hand in hand, had sought refuge in a church confessional. Their baby faces still wore that look of endearing innocence that only children know.

The exact reasons for the destruction of Oradour have never been established, but at his trial in East Berlin in 1983, Second-Lieutenant Barth, one of those under Major Dickman's command – and, at the time of the trial, a banally dressed pensioner – stated that, for him, the massacre at Oradour was a 'completely normal action'. He was sentenced to life in prison, after which he commented with chilling self-regard that he 'regretted that his prison sentence would not allow him to enjoy his grandchildren, as he had hoped'.

The ravaged site of Oradour-sur-Glane is an example of the concept of *lieux de mémoire* – sites embodying memories that would otherwise be swept away by history. Oradour has thus become emblematic of the many obliterative transgressions carried out by the German forces – and indeed by forces anywhere. Walking around the grey-hued village was like stepping into war-time newsreel. The buildings looked as though they had been bombed. At the tram station, some of the delicate blue ceramic tiles that had once named the village had survived. They spelled out ORA   G   E.

Orage means thunderstorm.

In the Centre de la Mémoire, I read that the Vichy government had replaced the Republican motto of 'Liberty, Equality, Fraternity' with that of the Vichy state: 'Work, Family, Motherland'. There was a sense that both mottos were honoured at Oradour. For, as I walked around, with the help of simple signs on the walls of the ruins, I conjured up a picture of a village that had once been industrious, self-sufficient and hospitable. Men had been massacred at a wine store, a forge, a bakery, a barn. In the smitten church, a plaque invited '*Reconnaissance à Sainte Bernadette, modèle de piété, d'obéissance de travail*'.

The SS looted the houses before setting them on fire, taking from them all they could carry. I assumed that what was left was what they could not carry or did not value: the weight of water troughs, pots, ironmongery, the chairs and tables from all the cafés. And the domestic remains: pans hanging or at rest on their sides, rusting sewing machines.

After the war, the fate of the village was given attention, but its survivors felt betrayed by the new government. When, in 1953, the court in Bordeaux – for political expediency – granted amnesty to those of the accused from Alsace who claimed to have been forced to join the SS, the mayor returned the Legion of Honour awarded to the village and refused to inter the ashes of the dead in the state monument. Instead, these were marked by a memorial raised by private subscription. Years later, the village and the state resolved some of the bitterness that had been felt, and now the state monument is a museum, housing some of the artefacts found after the tragedy: spectacles, dental instruments, broken glassware, scraps of material, a classroom's worth of pure white inkwells.

¶

In the former Resistance centre in the pine forest of Mont Mouchet, high in the rolling hills and woodland of the Margeride, stood a museum and a large, well-meaning monument, as tall as a small apartment block. There were also a few stacked cornerstones, which belonged to the former forest house where Resistance members once met. I arrived here late one afternoon, after passing through a landscape screened from me by high pines. The wind blew through them like an elegy.

I had been travelling unhurriedly back towards Saint-Flour, driving through a corridor of villages that seemed leached of life. A hasty judgment, perhaps, but as Robert Louis Stevenson writes in his essay 'An Autumn Effect', 'A country rapidly passed through [. . .] may leave upon us a unity of impression that would only be disturbed and dissipated if we stayed longer.' I had set my nose for Aumont-Aubrac, but neither there, nor at Rimeize, Saint-Alban-sur-Limagnole, nor especially in Le Malzieu-Ville, could I find a place that attracted me enough to linger in it, to disturb my 'unity of impression'.

I stopped in Paulhac-en-Margeride, a village that had been torched by the German forces in 1944 and rebuilt after the war. Its one *auberge*, despite a sign reading '*Bienvenue*, Welcome', was closed on Sundays.

I walked to the centre of the village and visited the church. On the wall outside were three plaques honouring the bravery of Resistance fighters and those caught up in their actions. I wondered whether re-building could do anything other than honour good intentions.

The light was failing as I descended towards Saint-Flour. As the sun sank, the sky was marked by a striated red. A glow of green light hung over the rich rolling pastures below the narrow road. Soon, the darkening woods were finally black, impenetrable. The last light bled away as I passed through each Sunday-shuttered village; a huddle of roofs and an empty square, a closed café. It felt as though the road, sensible of the emptiness in each of these places, was rushing me by.

But the next day, in sunshine, I retraced the route, stopping off on a number of occasions to look at roadside monuments, which were mostly the size of large way-makers or small obelisks. This one was typical: '*Juin 1944. Ici tombèrent 2 héros de la Résistance*'. Thus, in the short distance between Clavières, a 'martyr village' with its mass grave of twelve unknown Heroes of the Resistance, and Mont Mouchet itself, the numbers were carved into stone – 2 fell, 3 fell, 9 fell, 13 fell.

The small monuments told of other qualities, ageing quietly behind the shuttered windows, that made it hard to tell if a village was sleeping or dying. This was a landscape with history, blood and memory. The looming armoire may indeed have terrified our sensitive boy, but it would be an error to underestimate the shelter a village gives or indeed of what it is capable. Out of these villages, these closed villages and this wooded landscape, had come courage, resolve and sacrifice.

In Another World: *Among Europe's Dying Villages*

Of Armoires and Wolves

Singer

On winter nights with something of a sigh
my mother brought in the sewing machine
and laid it on the living room table.
I remember the weight of it

as she put it down and its full-lunged shape
as she took off its cover and firelight
lit its flanks. For those moments no matter
what else I was doing I watched

her palm gently massaging the black wheel.
How little it took, yet how busily
that shining needle, worked as with cloth spread
between thumb and stretched forefinger,

she fed through the hem of a skirt
or a frayed trouser cuff, her expression
like someone forming first letters, their pen
dipped in a white well of dark ink knowing

the slightest loss of concentration now
and the work is likely ruined. And when
the machine was done, there'd be the faintest
glow of pleasure fanning her cheeks

as she lifted her face; returned to us
garments needing no more now than a brush
of the iron. In Oradour,
when the killing was done, they looted all

they felt was of worth. The rest they condemned
to fire. Along desolate streets, in house
after house, among the discordant clefs
of rusted chairs and table frames,

the rims of lived life that the fire has left,
the sewing machines remain. They graze now
on rubble or perch on their birthing stands.
They have still the pleasing bovine

swell of their hindquarters: but their heads
are bent like beaks, ready for work.

A Village History of Europe

there is a common field
in the centre of a village

one half of the village
does terrible things there

it is the duty
of the other half to remember

we cut off the hair
and then we remember

we stack the shoes
and then we remember

we say walk into this well-lit room
and then we remember

we put our fingers to our lips
and then we remember

then we forget and the grass grows
on both sides of the field equally

In Another World: *Among Europe's Dying Villages*

Fair Exchange

It was late September; the trees had turned, the chestnuts had already fallen. He had arrived in a village in the Auvergne and booked into a country inn, a so-called '*hôtel de charme*'. Such a designation, he had noticed, was one of the myriad ways in which the French created a sense of exclusivity. It was reminiscent of the Irish habit of awarding plaques to pubs with the loosest linkage to James Joyce. He'd encountered plenty of those when researching *Historic Pubs of the Emerald Isle*.

This village had been named 'one of the most beautiful villages in France', another anointing. A leaflet he'd picked up at the hotel informed him that its 'extraordinarily rich historical heritage' extended back to medieval times and that it had once been home to Benedictine nuns. 'Tucked away at the end of a narrow valley, its isolation has saved it from the ravages of time. Its character is waiting to be discovered at each corner of its picturesque lanes.' (He could use all of that.) As darkness was falling, he took a walk through these lanes, noticing the buildings that had already benefited from a new stream of money and those others still boarded up in darkness.

In an empty bar on a corner, he fished coins – from among a handful of the chestnuts he had gathered – to buy a glass of red wine. The middle-aged woman serving him, one dress strap falling off a shoulder, appeared distracted with tiredness. She tipped the bottle upright once before putting the glass down hard on the counter. A trace of wine gathered at the base of its stem. Through the door in the back wall of the bar, he glimpsed *le patron* in the kitchen, sleeves rolled up at the table, a bottle of wine before him. A raucous soap opera was contesting the family conversation. Not much to recommend this place, he thought.

Still, he idled before a handful of old photographs of the village on the salon walls. In them, he saw some of the same cracked doors and worn steps he'd just passed, but with solid and serious black-clad figures posed before them. This was the hour – *entre chien et chat* – when you might apprehend some ghostly sense of what the village had been

117
Fair Exchange

like when it was truly a working village. Yet the photographs sent him into a momentary wave of free-floating melancholy. Gloria. In all those dark Irish bars, she had shone – her hazel eyes, the highlight of a rogue shaft of light on her hair. Now, here he was in another dark bar, with the reflection of his face on the glass of the photographs staring back at him with a haunted look.

He finished the wine – cold, metallic, sharp – and passed the doors and steps again, the shadows now deepening, but the sky clear, the stars glittering.

¶

His room back at the hotel was in a part of the building that swelled into what had once been a grain store. Its walls were three feet thick, its floor was tiled, and, in the night, cold grew there like ivy. It twined over his shoulders and feet until his intermittent sleeplessness turned into full wakefulness. But it hadn't just been the cold. He'd found his thoughts drifting towards the figure of a willing girl, with almond eyes and a mane of cropped black hair. It had felt like a betrayal.

At first, in mild irritation, he switched the light on. The room that had looked so atmospheric, as the afternoon sunlight fell across the floor from its small deep-set window, now seemed like a cell to him. He searched for heating and found none. In the clinical bathroom, the towel rail was so cold it burned. He hunted through the wardrobe and chest of drawers for a blanket. Once, many years before, back when his travel-writing career consisted of no more than sending in updates to the *Rough Guides*, he had shivered through a night in Brazil before going to see the falls at Iguaçu. When he had complained the next day, the hotel owner had opened the wardrobe door and waved his hand at two thick woollen blankets. He didn't want to repeat that embarrassment. But there were no blankets to be found here.

He lay, hunched into the bones of himself, and resolved that he would not pay the full price. He had a fair idea of how he'd like the conversation to go, and he rehearsed it in his head until the early morning light edged through the shutters.

He rose and showered, the warmth of the water sluicing away the cold through a stylishly bevelled drain. There was a heaviness behind his eyelids, but he was pleased the ordeal of the night was over.

He went downstairs and attracted the attention of *la propriétrice* with a small wave. She was busy setting tables for breakfast in the dining area. There was no one else in the foyer, which was a relief, as he certainly didn't want to make a scene. He'd rehearsed a few phrases in French and was confident that she would agree to a greatly reduced tariff, if only to protect the reputation of her *hôtel de charme*. Then, he hoped, she would invite him through to *le petit déjeuner*. Already, he could smell the coffee.

But the omens were not propitious. From behind the reception counter, she regarded him with something like exhaustion herself as he told her how badly he had slept, that there were no extra covers in the room. And the towel-rail heating in the bathroom had not been on either.

'No, it wouldn't have been. The heating's not turned on until the end of this month.' She said it with no hint of an apology. He told her bluntly he did not want to pay the full price.

'*Ah, non,*' she bridled. 'You will pay, *monsieur.*'

He told her he wanted to pay what was due, but not the full amount. 'When I come to a hotel, I expect warmth, not to be unable to sleep because of the cold. And I should inform you that . . .'

'No, *monsieur,*' she insisted, 'you will pay.'

Her eyes were hard now, her jaw set, and he wondered if she saw him as some vagabond trying to evade payment altogether. No one *else* had ever complained before, she said.

'Look, the money's not important to me,' he said, lapsing into English. 'It's the principle of it. You know, the ancient barter between innkeeper and traveller. In return for a warm bed, I'll pay a reasonable rate: fair exchange. That's the basis of movement and pilgrimage. Who cares how chic your hotel is – I was cold!'

His sudden wave of righteousness seemed to have the same effect on her as it used to have on Gloria.

She flicked a hand in anger through her hair and flipped open her book of bills. She repeated that he would pay the full amount, and the demand lay in the silence between them.

Fair Exchange

After half a minute or so, she spoke. 'All right, you don't have to pay for dinner. But for the room, yes.'

'For dinner?' he said. 'But that was hardly anything.'

'You had *fromage*.' She spat the word as if disgusted by it and carefully began to Tipp-Ex out the item on his bill.

¶

He had not felt hungry all day and had returned from his cold glass of wine feeling no more than peckish. He'd begun to cast an eye with mild interest over the menu pinned to a splendid lime tree on the small terrace of the hotel.

A girl appeared at his shoulder: raven-black cropped hair, soft oriental features. 'Will you be eating, *monsieur*? We stop serving at eight-thirty.' It was already quarter past. He spotted a '*sélection de fromages auvergnats*'.

'Would it be possible simply to have cheese?' He was aware of a coquettish pleading in his voice.

'*Bien sûr, monsieur.*'

'And a glass of red wine?' There was that involuntary voice again.

'*Bien sûr.*'

He took a seat on the terrace. There was a couple rounding off their meal with coffee and brandies. No one else.

She brought him four wedges of cheese arranged on a plate and three pieces of bread, still light and fresh, in a basket. A glass of warm, velvety red wine.

'Would you like salad with it?' Her eyes sparkled. This, he thought, was what you paid for.

The salad arrived in a small white bowl. Simplicity itself. The lettuce was the kind of green that appears to emit light, the green of everything at its most fresh and perfect, the lambent 'green fuse' itself. Its crispest leaves were at its centre and it was dressed in a lemony oil.

'Oh, *parfait*,' he said. '*Parfait*,' and the soft lantern of her face smiled down on him.

'Your name?' he asked as innocently as he could.

'Xin,' she replied, then spelled it out for him, with deliciously small movements of lips, teeth and tongue. 'X-I-N.'

¶

It had been during a hot day in June that Xin had first slipped under her employer's single white sheet. The lunches had all been served and cleared. A few diners still lingered under the chestnut trees, unwilling to make anything else of their day.

For weeks, Xin had seen what she thought of as neediness beneath Madame's brusque exterior. Then one night, as Xin was reaching for a bottle of Lafitte, Madame had laid her hand on the top of Xin's wrist. It was simply to guide her, the most natural of gestures, but it had caused Xin to turn her clear greenish eyes towards her and smile. Madame dipped her head in embarrassment, as if to acknowledge, with surprise, that her gentle touch might have carried another meaning.

As for Monsieur, he was never there. He worked in Paris, though it had been from Paris that he'd drawn his wife down to this village – this backwater that depended on tourism for a lifeline. It was to be their big break from city life, their opportunity to spend some time together. But the first year had not been as profitable as he'd hoped. He would have to go back to his old job in the capital.

'You can do that?' she'd asked.

'Yes, they always said that if it didn't work out here . . .'

'And you let me think that we were both in this together. Total commitment, wasn't that the phrase?'

'And it still is, of course it is. But I'll make far more money back in the office, and we can find someone to help you run things here in high season.'

It would be fine, he'd said. The TGV to Clermont and then a drive down. He'd make it most weekends. And when it got quiet down here, she could come up to Paris. Thank goodness they hadn't sold the apartment in the Marais. They were lucky, in fact, that they didn't have children. Weren't they?

But it hadn't quite worked out like that. There were work functions and conferences and immoveable dates. And sometimes he was just too exhausted to make the journey.

'You know I *want* to, you know it's true. I'm just too tired.'

She knew that well enough. Even when he made it down, he was often *too tired*. She'd turn from him and stare at the fresh white walls and wonder what her life had become. Like the village in which she was imprisoned, she felt neither quite dead, nor yet with a life she could call her own.

Xin lived in Paris most of the time too, near the Gare de Lyon. She was studying fine art, but needed a summer job. And needed to get away from her family. The Monsieur had found her neat, intelligent and apparently competent. He told his wife it had been an easy appointment to make. He had interviewed her in Paris, then she'd travelled down.

She was wearing a sarong in the heat and she'd brought a tray with a jug of iced water and two glasses. She'd knocked softly on Madame's door.

'It's so hot this afternoon. I brought water.'

'Oh, well, wonderful.' And Madame had laughed at the boldness of this girl.

She sat up, pulling the sheet around her and pinning it with her arms. For a moment, Xin just stood there. With her spiked black hair and her slim body, she could almost have been a boy.

'Just put it there,' Madame said vaguely.

Xin sat on the edge of the bed, laid the tray on the floor and poured two glasses of water. The glasses beaded with condensation.

'Delicious,' Madame said. 'Delicious.'

It had seemed the most natural thing in the world, on that clammy afternoon, to ease herself over on the king-size bed to let Xin lie beside her.

'So hot,' said Xin and unwrapped herself. They both laughed as they kicked the single white sheet till it billowed like a sail. The air too was now delicious, charged.

Throughout the summer afternoons, Xin would bring a jug of iced water and two glasses to her employer's room. Xin's young, smooth body, so understated in its sexuality, but each part of it wonderfully alive, had revived something in Madame that she'd thought deeply buried. And without straining to, or giving thought to it, she discovered that she too could feel and give pleasure again, just by *being*, by doing what came without thought and was met without judgment.

Xin began to bring oils to the room and would massage these into the knots she found around Madame's neck and shoulders. And then Madame would massage Xin's body, inexpertly, but getting to know the firm thighs, the small interruptions of her breasts, the blue-black aureoles of her nipples.

'Oh, what will I do when you leave?'

Xin said nothing to that. There were only two weeks left before she had to return to Paris. The village had been a pleasant place to pass the summer months, but she was excited about the courses she had chosen for the coming semester, particularly one on Art and Gender, delivered by a lecturer whose special area of research was Camille Claudel, the doe-eyed and mournful mistress of Rodin.

'My very dearest, I'm down on both knees before your beautiful body, which I embrace,' Rodin had written to his lover. Xin had sat and studied a photograph of her long and hard. In Xin's eyes, Claudel could have been Rodin's equal as a sculptor, but the separation had broken her, led her eventually to madness. Nowadays, Xin was sure, everything was different; nothing so tragic could ever possibly happen.

What did Xin's silence mean? wondered Madame. And how had it come to be that she knew so little about her? Most of her questions were treated with a little laugh of unimportance. And yet Xin knew all about *her* situation. She'd even met her husband and had charmed him into getting this job. On a couple of his visits to the village, Xin and he had exchanged a few words.

'How amusing,' she'd said later. She had a way of saying things that, at the time, seemed of no importance – flip, throw-away comments that Madame found herself brooding over afterwards. Amusing? What was so amusing? And when? How had her husband met Xin anyway?

Their lovemaking took on a new, violent edge. There was no massaging now, no sweet oils, only a frantic clash. It seemed sometimes that what she really wanted to do was to rip Xin, limb from limb, to pull her buttocks apart like you would a peach. Xin gave no sign that she found any of this distasteful. Quite the opposite, and Madame had to censure her, reminding her that her husband would question any weals he found on her body.

Madame began to feel that the overpowering tiredness that was overcoming her, even when she had slept well, was a result of being drained by Xin. She'd once read a Chinese folktale about a fox that could change form into a seductive girl and exhaust the life force of her victim. And Xin had not only the habits of a fox, thought Madame, but the musky, sweet smell as well; there were times when she was sure she felt the quick swish of a silken brush among the many softnesses during their afternoons in bed. And other times when she imagined Xin gnawing at the blind nub of her like a fox upon a bone.

But in contrast to the desperate violence of her lovemaking, there were also the secret and tender touches she stole at other times, brushing her hand against Xin's neat buttocks, stroking a hand, seeking a thigh beneath a table. Xin would smile at her if she could. Nevertheless, her own suggestiveness began to feel unbecoming. Wasn't it just another sign of her desperation, the imbalance she felt? Yet, for her life, she could not stop it.

She began to resent seeing Xin carry out the very tasks she'd been employed to do. The way she smiled at guests, no differently from the way she smiled at Madame, the way she met their desires, the way she pleased. That light and easy laugh. And, standing at her bedroom window, as she watched Xin going out of her way to solicit a tall middle-aged man, all bony angles, reading a menu in the fading light, she felt the icy resentment begin to grip her heart with renewed force. With every small act, Xin added to his delight. In his flushed cheeks, the way he stretched his neck towards her like a hungry goose, she saw her own gullibility, her own blindness.

Before she went to turn the heating off in his room, a little ashamed of her own pettiness, she was aware of her face contorting in disgust at his display.

¶

He had eaten slowly, ruminatively, savouring the cheeses. Each was marked by its own consistency, its own accent and tone. One resisted his knife more; one, blue-flecked, tended to crumble; another parted neatly when sliced. There was creaminess, nuttiness, sharpness – each finding different tastebuds and sending waves of pleasure through his body. This was the *terroir* singing to him its first songs: Cantal, Sainte-Nectaire, Gaperon, Bleu d'Auvergne. He decided he would devote a whole section of the new book to cheeses.

As he ate, not in a glut of hunger, but with enough edge taken off his appetite to ensure thoughtful appreciation, as if this final course had created a ghost meal before it, he knew it had been a meal without price. He thought of the handful of such meals he'd had in his life that had become engrained in his memory. Most had been the simplest fare – mackerel from Luce Bay cooked over a charcoal fire, potatoes in the Andes baked in the earth, the golden soufflé Gloria had once conjured from his near-empty fridge.

¶

Without price. And yet, there it was now, the price, written in neat black writing that grew fainter with each white stroke. He felt himself weakening.

He retained enough bile to place his notes on the counter and to bid her as cold a goodbye as his night had warranted. As she returned his *au revoir*, he caught something in her of the fragile haughtiness of one of the Benedictine abbesses who had once been the autocrats of the village. The abbess had recognised 'no authority temporal or spiritual other than that of the Pope'. He saw now, with satisfaction, that there was something about *la propriétrice* of the abjurer, the vow-maker. But, whatever lonely authority she assumed, she would never know how, as the day progressed, his spirits lifted and tiredness fell from his eyes. Meanwhile, he passed through a string of shuttered villages no nomenclature gave any sign of saving and, like every other traveller, he took no note of any of them.

In Another World: *Among Europe's Dying Villages*

Gift from the Sea

She would never forget the first night she saw the village. It seemed to hover in the darkness over the plain. It was a wonder to her then, its lights like bright pockets of honey scattered through a hive. Only as she drew nearer did she see the dark hull it was built on.

They'd found her on the beach, her dress clinging to her, sand through her black hair, her face cold as marble, and they'd thought her dead at first. But her chest had heaved when they worked it and the seawater gurgled out. They carried her into the marina and put a blanket over her. She gave them a name, Zerya; they made a tag of it. She shook her head at every other question. Zerya. One of the lucky ones. They were given soup and hot drinks, and one of them broke from a bow-backed group to tell her that her brother wasn't with them anymore.

Antonio had been called for because the storm had damaged the electrics and they needed someone to fix up a temporary generator. He looked down on her and saw someone in the glare of the sodium lighting like one of the saints in its glass case – Santa Monica or Santa Brigida – pale, smooth, lost somewhere in the thoughtful stages between life and death.

She wanted to sleep forever when she remembered what had happened. How the packed boat had lunged one way then another in the storm, how people had moaned and cried out to be saved or had pressed into each other wordlessly. Then she recalled the great wave coming at them, like a wall of flame, and how it had ripped her from the boat deck, torn her from her brother, his eyes still wide and fierce with life, and hurled her into the sea. There was no more thinking after that, no fear of what would be lost or what was to come – just the body reacting to its circumstances, her limbs thrashing, with or without hope, her mouth ready for the breath that might save her.

When she heard the name of the village that night, it was all vowels to her, and when they said it to her over and over, as she asked them to, it sounded like a lullaby.

'What is to happen to them all?' Antonio asked.

The Carabinieri shrugged.

¶

After a few days, an official position had been taken. It was decided that those who wished to stay on to look for work in the village could do so. Villagers were encouraged to think of work that might be suitable. It gave rise to heated arguments among the men in the Bar Centrale in the old hilltop village, some of whom had never even heard of the place where they'd been told the boat people had come from.

'How will people like that fit in here?'

'Yes, people washed up by the sea.'

'They don't even speak our language.'

'Look, you have eyes in your head, don't you? The village is dying. Dying. When was the last wedding you were at?'

'I can't remember. But I was at Paolo Giovanni's funeral last week.'

'Funerals. Pah! Ten a penny. Isn't it clear that what this place needs more than anything is people? Look on what the sea has given us as a gift.'

'A gift that doesn't understand us.'

'Nor we them.'

'They can learn to speak our language.'

'As long as they don't expect us to learn theirs.'

'Well, after all, a donkey can only say hee-haw.'

'What's that you say?'

¶

Zerya was a quick learner. At least of the few lubricating expressions that help someone to get by. It was her use of such expressions that persuaded Antonio's mother to take her on. Widowed for ten years, she had turned the small farm her husband had run into an *agriturismo* business – accommodation in the big old farmhouse and a restaurant in a converted outbuilding. Little traffic passed the sign they'd put on

In Another World: *Among Europe's Dying Villages*

a bend in the road, halfway between the marina and the old village, so business was slow. But Antonio's mother thought she could try the girl for a while. She could change beds and clean rooms and, in the evening, work in the restaurant where Antonio served. That would allow Antonio to work more hours as an electrician, which paid considerably better. It was said in Bar Centrale that Antonio's mother would have had him working night and day if she could.

What his mother liked to do best was to stand on the terrace with a huge pair of binoculars, watching for movement in the valley and the plain below. She could spot a strange car coming up the winding road or workers slacking in the olive groves that swept down over the plain to the coastal village and to the sea beyond. In fact, she claimed to have been the first to see the ship in trouble that night, saw its faint lights go out and, even in the rain-driven blackness, saw the huge white-top that capsized it and the dancers from the marina that came to the water's edge to help the survivors. This was perhaps the most extraordinary of the claims that had already earned her the nickname of 'Grandma Eagle'.

Sometimes, to impress visitors, Grandma Eagle would ask them to point to some part of the village down below – a shop or a bar that was a mere blur, even through her binoculars – and she'd read the name of it, even read the sign outside.

'There,' she'd say. 'Eh, there.'

But of course the visitors would know she'd memorised the names over the years. There were not so many to learn, and where else, after all, had she been? Still, visitors like to please, so they would act with surprise and she'd jab another 'Eh' at them, to make sure they were taking her seriously.

'Ask up in the village who has the keenest eyes around here. They'll tell you.'

The first time she tried it with Zerya, pausing between each gobbet of deciphered information – 'Hotel Bar Marina: Special today, *spaghetti al pomodoro*' –, Zerya nodded enthusiastically. But when she lifted the binoculars again, Zerya and Antonio exchanged glances and smiled. How easy it had felt to betray his mother! His mind kept returning to this briefest of conspiracies throughout the following day as he worked in the old village.

Antonio liked his work. What else was there here for him? The olives, that was about all. Much of his trade was at the edges of the village, before it fell away into roofless husks. That was where the occasional house was being renovated, given new life. When he was in the cool, dusty near-darkness there, he felt the village was almost animal above him; here he was, burrowing away into its soft underside, bringing light and energy. He was not a small man, but he had found ways to fold himself into unlikely places – corners, attics, foundations – and when it was all going smoothly, he felt that the village itself had almost rolled away, like a big cat, to let him do his work.

What he wanted, he realised soon after meeting her, was to live in the village, but not to feel its pull on him, that terrible inertia, that stasis. With one glance and a smile, Zerya had ripped through layers of custom and let in a little air. She would bring him both air and light: he would have two lives here, and she would be the centre of the second one.

Others seemed to have similar ideas, for Zerya was beginning to be an attraction at the restaurant. The men who frequented it now went home first to wash the work-dust away, to change into white shirts and to shave the stubble from their cheeks. They turned to watch her as she came from the kitchen carrying plates of lamb shanks or cuts of beef. Sometimes they chose to sit close to the kitchen for the chance to have a few words of small talk with her. At other times, they broke years of custom and sat at the far end of the empty room, the longer to watch her return to the kitchen again, their eyes on her bare calves, her shoulders.

There were still moments, when she felt a warm brush of air on her shoulders or the light too brightly shaping them, that she would feel a quiver of doubt passing over her skin and hear her father's voice chastising her. But with confidence, and language, came a studied irreverence towards these men with their broad, hairy forearms, their willing smiles. No longer with downcast eyes, she took to contradicting their orders, telling them what she would recommend or urging them to try something new.

'Signor, you've had pork the last three times. Try something different. Only sheep eat grass all the time.' Her smile disarmed her customer before his eyes could darken.

Or she might say, 'Who knows, signor, when a life will be cut short? Pity to go to heaven with so many tastes unknown.' But this she'd say so sadly that their eyes would lower to the menu once more.

Antonio, coming from work, grimy and tired, would stand in the darkness outside and watch her and the eager diners. In her presence, even they, he noticed, seemed to bristle with fresh hope.

¶

She made the bed and looked out at the view. The twists of olive trees, the red roofs, the fan of turquoise sea that covered the sand before it deepened into a rich ceramic blue. It was beautiful, of course. She could see that, now the sea didn't terrify her anymore, although she hadn't touched fish since and probably never would. But despite a flicker of fear above the sadness that she knew would never shift, she was comfortable for the moment, smoothing sheets and sweeping floors. This routine world was enough for her – in fact, it was a blessing. And he, Antonio, was at its centre.

When her brother's bloated body had been washed ashore, his flesh flayed from it, great gouges where it had been nibbled and clawed, it was into Antonio's arms that she had fallen, Antonio looking down on her blenched face again. Yet, even faced with this most intimate of deaths, she had shaken her head at any further questioning about her past life.

Once, his mother had given her a lunch for Antonio and instructed her on where to find him. She climbed up, past the crumbling walls, to the piazza, where some of the refugees were huddled in the shade.

'Work,' they said. 'Where is the work? There is much we could do here. But who is to pay for it? The people are kind, but you can't live on kindness forever.' She saw small bitternesses begin to grip them and preferred not to spend too much time in their company. If she did, she knew what the conversation would come around to.

'And how can you walk around with your shoulders bare and your head uncovered? We have heard talk . . .'

She found the alleyway Antonio's mother had told her about and followed it down the shallow steps, through an archway, till she came to the building in which he was working. She noted how gracefully his body met the demands of the small space in which he had to operate, noted, when he said he'd be with her in a minute, how delicately his fingers worked in the small metal junction box. He turned from his work and smiled at her. She knew what fired such a smile and felt briefly uneasy as she held out his plastic lunch box.

One afternoon, in room number four, Zerya was changing sheets. Antonio said he had come back to fetch something for work and now that he was here he may as well help her. She shrugged that there was no need. He said he'd like to and, taking hold of the edge of one sheet, he ripped it from the bed and held it high above him, like a billowing flag, before letting it fall to the bare floor. He stood, smiling slightly, as if at a loss as to what to do next. Or perhaps this had been some kind of challenge?

She dragged the bottom sheet across the bed; then, to make her display the equal of his, she spun around, wrapping herself up within the sheet. She blushed at her silliness and a look of pain crossed his face. He took a few faltering steps around the bed, his eyes nervously attentive, like one of the village dogs, unsure whether it was due a pat or a stone.

'My arms,' she said. 'Let me free my arms.'

She lifted them above the sheet and they held each other and he kissed her, awkwardly, before they fell onto the stripped bed. She felt the hunger in him, but also his restraint – the warring pleasures of immediacy and delectation: his kisses on her shoulders, the small lick he took above her armpit, the delicate movements of his fingers as they found a passage through the sheet, and that learned, within its constraints, the way her belly sloped from the rise of her early pregnancy.

As if burnt, he withdrew his hand, and she, clawed back to the customs of her youth, sat bolt upright and shook herself, like someone coming out of a deep sleep.

'I had no idea . . .' Antonio began.

'How could you have? But can we simply lie for a while?'

'If you want.' He gripped his side, as if he'd been wounded, and waited, while the intimacy of that other world waned and the room recomposed itself – the sheen of the small table, the drip of the tap, the sunlight on the floor and the tangled sheet. How would he now remember these, he asked himself, and her among them?

She turned to him and began to ruffle and smooth the hairs on his forearm. Her voice was soft and steady.

'That night,' she began, 'that night . . .'

¶

They were already cold and hungry when the sky began to darken and the wind picked up. They had been in the small boat for eighteen hours, eating only what the traffickers had allowed them to take on board – some bread and honey and a flagon of water.

Her brother had set his face rigid as a ship's figurehead since they'd left for their new life – away from the oppressions and marginalisations, the lack of any possibility for change. A few weeks before, when she found out she was pregnant, her lover had said that he too would follow her and her brother. They would be married, start afresh. She had not believed him, but that had not changed her mind. She had tried to confide in her brother, but recognised how brittle he was, that he needed to concentrate his energy on leaving, on not looking back on his father, his friends. For her, it had been easier; the new life she carried made her feel supple compared to him, able to look both ways, with some tenderness and with a little hope.

When the thunder rolled and the first huge hailstones fell, her brother simply grew more rigid, doing little to protect his face and concentrating on the coastline. It was she who noticed the terror around them, the way the migrants gripped more fiercely what was precious to them – when some of them were found later, their fists had to be prised open to free a small bag of money, a pair of shoes.

All that was happening in the lonely universe that night was this boat pitching and tossing in its own hell. She knew she would either

Gift from the Sea

die or find land. She would never return, not after what had happened to her mother. When the great wave came that turned the boat over, it seemed to her, as she was torn from him, that her brother simply toppled into the water. But the embers of his eyes, even now, glowed at her out of the darkness.

The doctors, giving her a cursory examination, had missed the pregnancy. She had reacted violently to their ministrations. Because of the shock, they reasoned, a full examination would only lead to greater trauma. 'Her pulse is strong enough. Let her be.'

¶

Antonio kissed her forehead. At times, he had lost the drift of what she was saying, as she had lost the grip of her new language. But he sensed the tone, the loss and the determination, and he recognised the privilege that she was granting him, sharing what she had never shared, before it hardened into anecdote, layered itself in memory.

'What happened to your mother?' he asked.

'Some other time,' she said.

¶

As the months passed, those who had survived with her began to drift from the village, some for fear that their residence permits would not come through – they would rather survive in the black economies of the cities in the north or in the shanty towns around Naples or Rome; others because the cold nights were falling once more and the narrow alleys of the hilltop village were deserted and bleak. What was there here for them, after all? The olives. The land. That had not been what had fuelled their dreams. Stories filtered back to the village of richer opportunities in the north, how some of the younger ones even had hopes of an education. It was possible, they said, nothing more.

The shopkeeper commented to Antonio's mother one day when she was buying bread that it was getting harder to depend on Antonio. He seemed to be preoccupied with something or other. Still, it was no business of hers, she said. Antonio's mother thrust the bread into her basket and did not contradict her.

In Bar Centrale, as the last fly of autumn skittered around a window, one of the wags said to Antonio, 'So, Grandma Eagle, she who can read the names of ships rounding the Cape of Good Hope, can't see what's happening under her own nose.'

'And what would that be?' another said.

'Oh, I think that in the restaurant, there's a *dolce* only served to the head waiter.'

'Something cooking in the oven, you mean?'

Antonio stalked off and heard the guffaws follow him into the empty piazza.

Zerya became aware of his mother eyeing her covetously, trying to discern her motives at every turn. Nor was she ignorant of the looks that followed her now that she was regarded as more than an *extracommunitario*. The white-shirted men, realising their opportunity had gone as they saw the pregnancy advance, frequently came unchanged from work and insisted on regular seats and their own choices from the menu.

'It would be different,' Antonio told her, 'if we were married.'

'But,' she said, 'marriage is not the most important thing. We could leave the village together. The three of us.'

'But if it is love, it can be love here too.'

'But . . .'

'Too many "buts" now,' he said. 'I don't like "but".'

'Yes, I know.' She cocked her head one way, then the other, then smiled. '*But* . . . you do want me to be in a place where I can be myself, don't you?'

'And who might that be?'

She had tried to tell him weeks ago in room number four. In the barrage of wind, hail and waves, when the situation looked hopeless, she had vowed that if she and her baby survived – for she knew many would not – she would not resolve herself to living in a place where she knew neither of them could thrive. For the first few days, when she'd lain in the hall and flirted with a hope to die, that thought had clearly weakened. But she could see now that her doubt had been only

Gift from the Sea

the final tempering of her will. She had not come from the sea to lose herself in a dying village.

'Your mother?' Antonio said.

'My mother,' she repeated and her breath quickened. 'My mother . . .'

Always, afterwards, he would see it through two imaginations – hers and his own. For months, she told him, her mother had hardly spoken: indifferent to the failure of electricity, the fouled water pipes, the scraping together of enough to feed a family. Her father had problems of his own, problems over which he had no control. And now he was losing control of his own wife. It was intolerable. When she locked herself in the back room, he shrugged. Let her shut herself away. What good was she to him as she was? Then they smelled it, the kerosene, drifting through the hall. Zerya remembered a sound like a buffeting wind as she rushed to the door to find it locked, feeling the heat and hearing, behind the rising wind, a high humming sound, then a crash as her mother, in flames, toppled over into a glass cabinet. Her brother held her off as her father broke down the door, doused the flames on her mother's nakedly raw body. Zerya was never allowed to see or to hold her mother, so she'd had to imagine forever how the flames surrounded her, how the flesh peeled from her, what was left of her when she was buried.

Zerya looked up and saw Antonio frowning hard at her, trying to understand.

'A place where I can be myself.'

She had only a dim idea of the shapes that were possible for her. But she had felt them stirring in her when she walked past the fountain at the village end and took the rock-strewn track that led far above the village, the smells of thyme and fennel sweetening the air. In the high forest of birch and oak, the wind whispered to her warnings of what her life here might become. She would never feel settled here. But, for her child, there was a chance.

When the baby was born, a beautiful girl, they named her, for convenience, Patrizia. The village women brought her gifts – toys, clothes and a pram. They took turns in holding her – cooing over her big eyes, her shell-like, almost transparent ears, her tiny toes. They would have a real baby for the crib at the *festa di san Rocco* for the first time in years.

¶

Antonio watched Zerya pack the little she had and took her to the station, down that twisting narrow road. They were early, so they sat in the small station bar, bravely smiling and losing themselves in the morning news programme. Antonio went to the bar and, standing in a line of men, ordered a *caffè*. She watched him load it with sugar, the tiny cup in his large delicate hands, then stir it disinterestedly and down it in one. He walked out, though it was lightly drizzling, and looked along the rails, the grass growing between the sleepers, as if he were keener than she that she should not miss her train. Antonio, kind to the end.

Still, she was shocked when the train finally arrived on time.

'Patrizia,' she said.

Antonio nodded. 'My mother,' he said. 'In fact, the whole village . . .'

'I'll write,' she said.

In the morning light, she saw a tiny scar along his cheekbone she'd never noticed before. Something in him then reminding her of her brother.

¶

She wrote that her time in *agriturismo* had stood her in good stead. She had found work up in the north – a small hotel where no one was interested in papers, though her pay reflected the lack of them. Then, some months later, a letter arrived with a French stamp on it. She was in Paris. Paris, he almost laughed, Paris! Who knows, perhaps, if it worked out for her there, Patrizia might grow up to be a Parisian. But things were more complicated. She had found work in a burger place on the outskirts of the city, but there had been a crackdown on migrant workers – what she had feared in Italy – and, as one of those *sans papiers*, she had had to go underground. Like the Jews in the last war, she said. That was how people were talking about it.

What has the war to do with any of this? he thought.

The last letter told him she had been found, or had given herself

137

Gift from the Sea

up – there was an ambiguity he could not fix no matter how often he read over it – but thankfully she had been able to protect those in the 'Resistance' who had given her safe hiding. Always, she wrote, she had been lucky in her protectors. She was to be deported. The letter ended there. No good luck. No goodbyes.

Antonio, in room number four, Patrizia close to sleep over his shoulder, looked over the olive groves, the marina, to the calm sea; not a breath of wind on it. He remembered how Zerya had once told him that if you said the name of the village over and over it sounded like a lullaby.

Gift from the Sea

In Another World: *Among Europe's Dying Villages*

Still Life

The weight of a bone-handled knife
signifies more in human life
than our aesthetics ever can.

from 'New Space' by Derek Mahon

At the entrance to the village of Filignano, in the mountainous region of Molise in southern Italy, stood a wire sculpture of Mario Lanza in open-armed performance. '*La Voce del Nostro Paese che Attraverso l'Oceano*', read the proud inscription. The freedom of its gestures was negated by the fact that the sculpture resembled a cage in human form. It was Mario Lanza's father who had first crossed the ocean, though his son, like many second-generation immigrants, was not indifferent to his village heritage. In 1954, the great man responded to a personal invitation from the mayor to visit Filignano after he had finished filming *Seven Hills of Rome*. In the small Piazza Municipio, dominated by its church and an ancient oak tree, Lanza sang his heart out for what he liked to call 'the little people' – people of conservative faith and habit.

Inside the church were highly coloured statues in postures of piety or suffering, and outside, on the entrance noticeboard, the parishioners' capacity for giving – or for withholding – was meticulously noted. There were two such records: one for 'Offerings for Christmas Star 2006', and another for 'Offerings for Acquisition of Diesel Oil 2006'. Peering behind the 2006 Christmas Star list, which was taped to the outside of the glass, I saw that many named benefactors, sensitive surely to this very public display, had doubled their contribution from 2005.

Beyond Filignano, shrines interrupted the lush verges every few hundred metres. Each had a figurine and an altar with candles and fresh or dried flowers. Spiritually, one church notice informed me, this was the 'Land of San Pio da Pietrelcina'. Beatified in May 1999, the saint is known commonly and affectionately as 'Padre Pio'. A leaflet described him as 'the world's best loved Capuchin'. Throughout Molise, bars and restaurants showed photographs of a bearded man with bright brown eyes in an attitude that conveyed grace and wisdom. The faded colours of these old photographs added to the effect: a different quality of light surrounded Padre Pio. Statues of him offering a blessing were frequent in the mountain villages, though lately it had been rumoured that his purported stigmata in fact had come from a phial of acid smuggled into his closed monastery by a willing nun.

I left the 'main' road and took a narrower twisting tributary along a sun-spotted valley to the village of Pantano, where the tiny road ended. I parked in the shade of a tree's green wing and walked into the village, coming first to a row of houses with tall, latticed iron fences and warnings about the dogs that patrolled them. But past these signs of the living, and past the fading red post box, I arrived at the part of the village that was deserted and quietly crumbling. The shallow steps of its cobbled *vicolos* – alleyways – wound up into the soft *tufo* rock of the hillside and disappeared into pressing tangles of undergrowth. On one corner, in the overgrown verge, a twisted, green metal bench rested at an impossible angle: whoever once sat at this spot commanded a view of half the village.

It was not its position, however, but the bench itself that held me. What grips us as writers is an unclear, chancy business. There are, for example, those members of the 'miraculous' school of poets, who will not write unless they are moved to do so, while others actively seek out subject matter, sending their senses out into the world to see what they might return with. Yet the movement away from one subject and towards another is inextricably linked to temperament, experience and history. Part of the pull of the dying village for me lies somewhere in my personal history, circumstances and experiences, in my tendency to look backwards, in my fondness for contemplating what is old, used and worn. The rusted bridle-bit, which I found half buried on a Highland croft, I love, not simply for its perfect melding of form and function, but also for its history, for its long encounter with time; for what Czeslaw Milosz describes in 'A Treatise on Poetry' as the 'Hours of labour, boredom, hopelessness/ [that] Live inside things and will not disappear'.

I suppose the word that best captures what moves me here is one of those untranslatable words, the Japanese *sabi* – a celebration of that which is old and faded. At its heart, *sabi* carries the Buddhist sense of life's transitory nature. Most of my wanderings through dying villages have been accompanied by a feeling of *sabi*.

I pushed on a half-opened door and explored. This first house, gouged from the rock, consisted of a small barrel-vaulted room. A few objects clustered round the fireplace: even in abandonment, the hearth was a focus. It was crossed by a rusted bedstead, no doubt tipped out of the way when the building had been cleared of anything thought to be of worth. Close by were two remaining cooking pots and a twig switch, hiding in a corner. And, as is so frequently the case, there was one object for whose presence there could be no accounting: the metal wheel of a cart.

The late Roger Deakin, in his final book, *Wildwood*, wrote about the railway carriage he liked to inhabit from time to time. It was roomy enough for one, and Deakin described his temporary life there as 'camping'. Accounting for the particular freedoms that the place gave, he wrote, 'There's more truth about a camp than a house [. . .] because that is the situation we are in. The house represents what we ourselves would like to be on earth: permanent, rooted, here for eternity. But a camp represents the true reality of things: we're just passing through.' The abandoned streets of Pantano bore much the same message. A few low doors further on was where the vintner once plied his trade. Here, lying as close together as eggs in a nest, were three globed, round-bottomed bottles, covered in a patina of grape-blue dust. They reminded me of glass floats, beautiful objects stranded in uselessness, detritus the tide might leave behind in a seaweed-cushioned cleft of rock.

Bottles: in the recessed wall spaces of the buildings I peered into there were generally two or three, seemingly composed as thoughtfully and as subtly as the still-life paintings of the twentieth-century artist Giorgio Morandi, who worked in one room in the house in Bologna in which he was born. He used the same elements in his still lifes over and over again. He removed the labels from bottles and let the colour of his ceramics dull with dust and age. His contemplative art was, he claimed, designed to communicate 'a sense of tranquillity and privacy'. To achieve it, he would take 'weeks to make up [his] mind which group of bottles [would] go well with a particular coloured tablecloth'. Both Morandi and the Scottish painter William Scott reworked elements from a limited source. And both were admirers of the eighteenth-century artist, Jean-Baptiste-Siméon Chardin, whose ascetic still lifes presented, without sentimentality, and at a time when the still life was regarded as the least of the genres, the ordinary trappings of the kitchen.

Scott was born in Greenock, to a Scottish mother and an Irish father who struggled to support his large family with his work as a sign painter. Scott remembered his childhood world as 'a grey world, an austere world: the garden I knew was a cemetery and we had no fine furniture'. His still lifes in the post-war years were arrangements of pots and pans, eggs, fishes and bottles on a bare kitchen table. Unlike Morandi's practice, these two-dimensional forms were drawn from memory. 'The forms I use are the forms I see about me and the forms I have dreamed about since I was a child.'

Although he disparaged any seeking of symbolism in his work, seeing kitchen utensils as simply the elements out of which he made his pictures, it would be hard to avoid seeing a broad social comment in Scott's often rigorous aesthetic, especially when viewed against much European still life tradition in which the still life proclaims plenitude. The seventeenth-century kitchen table Frans Snyders presents to us groans with a massacre of swan, peacock, boar and pheasant, while one of Jan Davidsz de Heem's towering flower arrangements is as impossible – the flowers are taken from different growing seasons – as it is ravishing.

Scott, on the other hand, found 'beauty in plainness, in a conception which is precise. [. . .] A simple idea which to the observer in its intensity must inevitably shock and leave a concrete image in the mind'. For example, a single mackerel lying on a white plate. In this painting, the main part of the fish's body is supported by the plate, while its head and its tail jut over the black table surface. Its skin is bluish, and its scales are as much a tribute to paint as they are to nature, but there is something very dignified, almost sacred, in the offering. In all Scott's still lifes of the 1950s, components were sparse: one fish, two or three pears, a few green beans. His is a contemplative art of frugality, and it is the relationships between common objects that create drama – the encounter between pears and a dish, mackerel and a plate. This is what the natural world offers, taken within the human element. And we are drawn into a world, where what is most common to us – 'the little people' – has become the chosen material for art. Although the results are hugely sophisticated, the selected components – edited by memory – are neither sophisticated nor in any way cosmopolitan. This is the stripped-back material world of those with limited pockets and options – it could be representative of the world of the village, as much as it is of Scott's impoverished childhood.

In exploring his own iconography in this way, during the 1950s especially, Scott became part of another still-life tradition, not one of plenty, but one that favours what the art historian Norman Bryson terms 'the unassuming material base of life that "importance" constantly overlooks'. This is the genre of rhopography (as opposed to megalography, the depiction of encounters with history and gods) that Bryson characterises as asserting a view of human life 'that attends to the ordinary business of daily living, the life of houses and tables, of individuals on a plane of material existence, where the ideas of heroism, passion and ambition have no place'.

For all its perceived lack of grand ideas, the pull of the *rhopos* – the seemingly small and insignificant – is strong. The forms of still life, like the ones I encountered in the dead half of Pantano – the flagon, the jar, the pitcher – are ones that have survived, whole or in shards, through aeons of archaeological time. Bryson writes of the 'cultural pressures' that have created their archetypal forms, pressures 'as vast as those which in nature carve valleys from rivers and canyons from glaciers'. But we should also honour the more transient forms, like those which moved J. M. Synge to comment in *The Aran Islands* (1907):

Every article on these islands has an almost personal character, which gives this simple life, where all art is unknown, something of the artistic beauty of medieval life. The curraghs and spinning-wheels, the tiny wooden barrels that are still much used in the place of earthenware, the homemade cradles, churns and baskets, are all full of individuality and being made from materials that are common here, yet to some extent peculiar to the island, they seem to exist as a natural link between the people and the world that is about them.

What will not survive the decades, never mind the aeons, may also (briefly) bear the imprint of vast 'cultural pressures'. And, in the rough-hewn houses of Pantano, in the gloaming of those shrine-like alcoves, it was not creative composition and memory, but rather the incremental touches of time itself that had given the 'found' still lifes their unity; dust and light had brought the objects to inhabit their cobwebbed frames with equanimity.

¶

I descended the shallow steps back down the *vicolo* and entered a very different habitation, a house that had once been one of the grandest buildings in the village. It boasted a set of broad marble stairs, at the turn of which, on a small landing, there was another compelling found still life, consisting of an upright dining chair and stacked bundles of firewood, each tied with string. The chair was elegant, its lacquered back richly gleaming. A window behind on the stairwell flooded the objects with sunlight, binding them into something numinous. Beyond these objects, the stairs continued to the attic rooms, up a thick carpet of feathers and bird droppings. There was an alarming flap of disturbed wings and I turned back from the heavy air.

Nothing suggested why the chair and the firewood bundles occupied the same space, nor why they should be left there facing each other. I am tempted to say they were 'placed', because there was something of the installation about these objects, a 'meaning' waiting to be teased

In Another World: *Among Europe's Dying Villages*

out. This is, after all, how we approach deserted rooms or buildings or ruins. We enter them looking for a meaning with which we are already partly familiar. The pleasure then lies in constructing relationships between objects and, from such a relationship, to imagine a life or lives. What is most creaturely in us – the concerns of rhopography – invites us into the scene: *there* is the grate with the cooking pot; *there* are the remains of a table, a broken chair; *there* is where the bed might have gone. Given a few hints, we will discover ghosts, or briefly lend our ghostly presence to this inanimate drama.

In certain powerful instances, one object can represent the domestic whole. As I had discovered at the village of Oradour-sur-Glane, it was the sewing machines that spoke of familial intimacy. Or again, it can appear that some objects, scoured or scarred by time, like the recessed still lifes of Pantano, can give an aesthetic satisfaction that is impersonal yet accessible.

But the chair and the firewood. A carelessness that represented abandonment? Or a chance encounter from which I could make a meaning? Some connection in one of my mind's far-flung alcoves was niggling at me.

¶

As autumn began slowly to burnish its deciduous trees, all over Molise communities were preparing for winter. Wood was stacked in the spaces beside houses, under awnings and, when those were full, at the front of the house, creeping up the window-sides, so that some houses looked prepared for a siege. Certainly, winter in the mountains of Molise is hard. The buckled and cracked tarmac showed the effects of the extremes of weather, and the road signs, frequently pocked with idling target practice, warned that tyres should have chains on them. Wood, though, was something the region had in abundance.

In the Mainarde Molisane, it was not hard to find a vantage point from where, in every direction, all I could see was forest coating the mountains and the valleys. The density of Italian oak and beech had once made travel problematic in this region and had ensured, along with the mountain barrier of the Apennines, that the area remained cut off from the large centres of power in Italy. Now, the expanse of white firs around Pescolanciano is classified by UNESCO as a MAB (Man and the Biosphere) reserve, accounting for the signs proclaiming '*Divieto de caccia*' (Cutting forbidden).

It was not always so. The hilltop village of Scapoli, some miles beyond Pantano, was one of a number of settlements created in the ninth and tenth centuries by the will of the powerful Abbey of San Vincenzo al Voturno. The abbey granted land it owned to farm-workers, so that they would free it of wooded cover and make it fertile. Wilderness, in particular the forest, was held in dread in the Middle Ages, and in much of Europe thereafter, as the stories of the Grimms testify. One of the major developments in the sensibility of artists during the Renaissance was that they considered the natural world not simply as a backdrop to their religious paintings, but, as in Leonardo's great *Annunciation*, as an earthly stage suited to wondrous happenings.

And true enough, many of the wooded areas I passed through were very beautiful and felt not at all threatening, although wolves and bears still inhabit this region. The Italian oak is a more slender, lightweight tree than its English relation. Its leafage, in a mature wood, is at the highest third of the tree, so a lot of light still falls through the canopy to the forest litter. If there's a path, it's a very pleasant place to walk – though when the ground is rockier and drier, the trees are stumpier and the forest impenetrable. But there's not a more beguiling road than the one bordered by the sunlit edges of a forest of oak and beech.

Such is the road to Scapoli, and, from it, villages emerged startlingly from their green surroundings. Each sang a siren song. How will you reach me? What will you find here? For each, no matter how small, offered the tantalising outline of a castle, a church, or both.

'There are villages here,' the girl in the tourist office in the regional capital of Campobasso had told me, 'that have great history and great tradition, but there are only a few old people living in them now. It's very hard for them.'

Attempting to drive up to one of these, the gradient became more alarming with every turn, and there were a couple of heartbeats in which

I doubted my Fiat's straining ability to make it. The road narrowed further into little more than a pavement. To the right of it stood a house with two women beside it. One was very old, clad in black and baring her false teeth in a fixed, involuntary grin. The other, her daughter, I assumed, was the decisive one and, though she seemed to be deaf and dumb, waved a finger at me regarding the road ahead and indicated with a sweep of her hand that I must turn around and go back to whence I had come. There was no parking here, and no passage further on. They were the self-appointed Keepers of the Gate. Unfortunately, I couldn't quite see how I was going to turn. The younger guided me, fool that I had been, inch by inch, making encouraging noises to tell me that there was more room than my eyes were telling me.

I drove carefully back down the road, looking out over the great beguiling landscape of Molise – the villages built around their castles, clinging to mountainsides or crowning hilltops, their palaces built along spines of rock. It was hard not to think of the forest as the sea; at one time in history, it had receded a little, leaving these isolated villages. And it was not difficult to picture the powerfully fertile force that surrounded them, and which once had to be cleared to build them, one day closing over them again.

¶

The spark of that metaphor of the sea brought my thoughts to bear on a landscape which is the exact opposite of forested land – an area in which trees do not grow, a place where wood was pulled as a precious catch from the high tide.

The great echoing hall of the Blasket Islands Heritage Centre, built with an extravagant amount of EU funding, stands on the Dingle peninsula on the west coast of Ireland. It rises above the village of Dunquin, from where, across the sound, the island of Great Blasket looked to Seán Ó Faoláin like a great whale surrounded by her twelve young.

It would no doubt have amused Tomás O'Crohan, the greatest of the astonishing crop of writers from the Blasket Islands, to have such a conspicuous structure in mainland Dunquin of all places, whose inhabitants' rivalry with the islanders O'Crohan refers to so frequently in *The Islandman*.

The words the Blasket Islanders left – either written or transcribed – are the now uninhabited islands' most considerable legacy. A few of the islanders, including Tomás O'Crohan, Peig Sayers and Maurice O'Sullivan, produced books which together form a small and geographically precise library that must be unique in world literature. The spur to this flowering, Declan Kiberd makes clear in *Inventing Ireland*, came from the Irish nationalists' cultural interest in the *gaeltacht* and their belief that the most uncorrupted form of Irish was spoken in this region.

A life so close to the elements, so close to the edge in every conceivable way, somehow imbued the islanders' language with an elemental power. Their lexicon could be as fluid as the sea, as alert as Fate, as commodious as Death. Although J. M. Synge described the islanders of the west coast as 'strange men with receding foreheads, high cheek-bones and ungovernable eyes' and claimed that it was 'only in wild jests and laughter that they could express their loneliness and desolation', the scholar George Thomson heard something altogether different. When he first heard the Irish spoken by the Blasket Islanders, Thomson wrote admiringly: 'It was as though Homer had come alive. Its vitality was inexhaustible. Yet it was rhythmical, alliterative, formal, artificial, always on the point of bursting into poetry.'

I had visited the Heritage Centre fifteen years before and seen O'Crohan's proud face, lean as a peat brick, featured on one of many hoardings bearing inscriptions concerning island life and the sea, 'the great enfolding, ever-present sea'. But I had been struck by the fact that this grand centre, while airy as a cathedral, contained little of any substance at all: no artefacts, trophies, scraps of clothing – nothing to fasten the senses upon what had once been useful or blessed: the 'natural link' that Synge noted 'between the people and the world that [was] about them', appeared to have been erased. A note to a series of photographs taken in the 1920s made clear, as if in apology for this expensive, rhetorical emptiness, that 'The islanders left very little of

In Another World: *Among Europe's Dying Villages*

worth.' They were 'a poor simple people living from hand to mouth'. Hunger was never far away; and where there was a possibility of augmenting their diet, they took it: if they suspected crabs lodged in a crevice, they stripped off and dived for them. What little material they had, the Blasket Islanders employed until it was all used up. They wore clothes until they frayed and fell apart, and they used furniture until it broke beyond repair, and then, as the winds of the Atlantic battered the coast, they used it as firewood.

Their days were a shedding of all that had ceased to be useful. In the end, the language and the patterns they made with it were all they had left: Crab Reef, Cormorant Rock, Black Head. But countless more of the rocks they sailed by became nameless with their deaths.

I thought back to that chance 'installation' in the abandoned building of Pantano, the tension between the furniture and the firewood. The wood of the fine chair that had had a destiny of which the firewood could only dream; the bundles of kindling a reminder of the true reality of things: lacquered black though you are, they seemed to say to the chair, you are only wood as we are. And some winter night, perhaps, after we are gone, to keep a song alive, you too will blister and burn.

Walnut Gatherers

Saepinum, Molise, Italy

Three men moving with purpose
and thought below the broad skirts
      of two walnut trees – at times
      in their shadows, at others

out on the ancient silvery stones
of Saepinum itself. They keep
      a proper distance from each other –
      there's ample for each

wherever they are –
though now and again,
      for none of the three is a young man,
      one briefly stands and sways

his back this way and that
before he dips again to the task.
      Per il dolci, I am told
      with a smile. The windfalls they want

have already slipped
their black jackets and hardened
      in the September sun
      to a semblance of wood. I take my foot

to one on a stone slab. It turns
to crumbs and shards. But for the second,
      my weight is perfect: the nut,
      all its foetal lines intact,

lifts out like a gift. The three men
drift away when their bags are full,
        leaning into the fading light
        to balance the knuckled weight.

They pass an arid fountain
inscribed by he who would be remembered
        for services once rendered
        this ruined provincial town.

Per il dolci. How right on such a day
to make time for sweetness: to mark presence,
        sunlight, silence, with the rhythmic
        click of walnut on walnut.

In Another World: *Among Europe's Dying Villages*

Twelve Red Roses

I was in Sydney, staying with a noted lawyer and his wife. I spent the days in the libraries, studying how the early colonists' views of Australia, its flora and fauna, its inhabitants, even its light, had been blinded by cultural determinism. In the evenings, I socialised with my hosts. One night – the evening of St Valentine's Day – we were invited to dinner at the house of their friend, Adriano. They told me he was keen to meet me. Adriano will do you proud, they said. He loves to cook for people. And his house!

His house was located on a spit of land overlooking the Harbour Bridge – a picture-postcard view. Fraser's wife, Pat, went ahead, while I lent him my arm. Fraser's sight was failing and his legal practice was sustained by memory and experience. We walked step by step to the front door, past a four-wheel-drive Jeep and a sports car in the open garage, past a pond with giant carp shimmering in the clear water. But for all its extravagance, there was something inescapably middle American and suburban about the house.

Adriano's daughter, Kaia-Lise, was at the door to greet us. She was fifteen and very beautiful – sallow skin, eyes dark as chestnuts, raven hair and a sullen insouciance that was only marginally held in check. We were told, soon after our arrival, that a dozen red roses had been sent to her that very day. 'Not the faintest idea,' she said, 'a mystery,' and everyone trilled.

Three Chinese servants stood behind her, two young women and a man, to whom we were not introduced. They moved to the side, opening like a human hinge, as we entered a marble-floored hall. Clearly, money had been lavished on its design and its execution, but again the result was mundane, more reminiscent of hospitals and grand toilets than tasteful living.

The dining table was set simply with cutlery and glasses, and a longer table at the head of the hall was laid with a spread of food. Before it, placing and fussing over the dishes, was Adriano.

'Ah, my friends, my friends.' He wiped his hands on a cloth and tossed it to one of the servants. 'Come. Come.'

I was introduced to him and he acknowledged me with a couple of nods.

'Sit. Sit. We must eat.'

Adriano was in his late fifties, large-featured and full of energy. His arms swelled from his shirt; a glisten of sweat was on his chest and on his imperious, balding forehead. I thought of the old film star, Edward G. Robinson, who could play tough when required, but whose solidity could belie a sheltering sensitivity. After our introductions, Adriano resumed his preoccupation with arranging and checking food, swapping a bowl of broccoli with a plate of ham, stirring butter and herbs through the potatoes.

'Eat! Eat! Before it gets cold!' But already much of it was lukewarm. The broccoli was overcooked and crumbled when I spooned it onto my plate. The spread was, I suppose, what you'd call hearty peasant food – stuffed peppers standing in pools of oil, lamb shanks, grilled fish. There was little conversation. Adriano ate, his eyes darting around the table, as we smiled at each other and took every opportunity, when his back was turned, to lighten the seriousness of the affair with short riffs of laughter.

'But I thought he wanted to meet me,' I whispered to Pat. Pat was blonde and birdlike and ever ready to laugh, though I'd heard that, in court, she was every bit as tenacious as her husband. It was tenacity, she said, that had landed him.

'I thought so too,' she smiled. 'But you never know with Adriano.'

I was restless. I had read enough now to want to exercise a few ideas. I was toying around with a title for the paper I was going to write: 'Cultural Determinism and Colonial Life' or 'Through a Glass Darkly: Natural Perception in the Early Days of Botany Bay, 1788–1850'. The latter title had only come to me as we were driving round the floodlit bay earlier that evening. I had wanted to share my excitement with someone.

After a few minutes, Adriano scraped his chair back and disappeared into the kitchen. We heard him shouting. Kaia-Lise hovered around, picking apart the occasional dolma, biting individual grains of rice in half, as if the shock of twelve red roses arriving had taken away her appetite. Adriano emerged from the kitchen, shaking his great bull head, while the three servants, clearly the objects of his wrath, trotted out after him with plates of rice pudding and baklava, untroubled by his rage.

We were joined by Yolanda, Kaia-Lise's tutor, a woman in her sixties. Her luxuriant grey hair, pulled back from her face, exploded from a clasp at the nape of her neck. Her face thrust itself at us – fierce brown eyes, fleshy lips and nose. She expounded her child-rearing belief: never trust a girl until she can earn money and pay for everything herself. Until then, what is her word worth? With what will she back it?

'Eh, even you, my precious, you with the twelve roses.'

Kaia-Lise flicked her hair grandly and pouted out a puff of air, designed to show that already her mind had moved a galaxy away from twelve red roses arriving anonymously on the front-door steps.

'Ah,' bellowed Adriano, as if in pain, 'I wanted champagne. Champagne first.' He pushed himself out of his chair and returned from the kitchen with two bottles. 'Oh, Adriano, champagne!' we all chirruped.

Adriano poured the champagne, his brows knotting with irritation at the bubbles as they built in each glass. He checked to ensure they were all full, then castigated us for not drinking.

'Drink,' he said. 'Drink!'

I thought I would try a toast, as a way of marking my presence and appreciation, but it fizzled out on Adriano's deaf ears. We clinked glasses ourselves. I felt a niggle of laughter beginning as Adriano rose again.

'Eat lamb like this. Like this. With fingers.'

We laid our knives and forks down and Fraser felt blindly for one of the small white bones.

'Ah,' we said, 'A-ha,' as if Adriano had unlocked some mystery for us we would never forget.

The meal eventually exhausted itself and the servants cleared the plates away. We were swept over to seats around a glass coffee table. Adriano's photograph album lay there waiting. I would have appreciated another glass of wine, but as far as Adriano was concerned we had finished eating and drinking. Now it was time for the photos.

Yolanda excused herself.

Here was Adriano in the Peloponnese, wearing a dark suit, with his mother beside him, about to leave his village. Here he was just arrived in Sydney, considerably slimmer than the huge man he was now. In both photos he was wearing the same suit. There were brothers and a sister in the photographs too, but it was to Adriano our eyes were drawn, because he was the one focusing on the camera, he was the one who knew the significance of each occasion. In the photo of himself back in the village on a visit, with his mother and his father in their wrinkled black clothes, there was his pride in both where he had come from and in the distance he had travelled.

'And your brothers?' I asked. 'Your brothers?'

Adriano looked somewhat irritated with the question. 'Back home. They tried, but they could not settle. Is not for everyone.'

He flicked through more pages – a car trip across Australia, Adriano with a couple of girls on a beach, playing the all-Australian boy – until he came to a photo of himself and his first wife. By this time, he was already established and working hard at his packaging business. You could see how carefully trimmed his moustache was, catch the confidence in his eyes.

Fraser had legally freed him from his second marriage. Not from the first – that wife was limp and exhausted – but from the second, the one that had marked his arrival among Sydney's serious players. His second wife had been considerably younger than him and vicious in adversity. She had left him for someone nearer her own age. The daughter she had left behind, Kaia-Lise, was now the only woman in Adriano's life. There was little that she was denied – a private-school education, violin lessons, designer labels, the latest mobile phone. Yolanda was employed to teach her Greek and, with a nod to his own weakness, to somehow protect the girl from the extremes of her father's generosity. Of his other daughters, one was in London, a corporate lawyer, the other a banker in New York. Global sophisticates, beneficiaries of Adriano's grip on the New World.

Adriano, though, was a man who did not easily forget. He brought the custom of his village life into the heart of cosmopolitan Sydney. When Fraser had suffered a stroke, Adriano had turned up at the hospital every day. He felt, along with those nurses Orwell describes in *Homage to Catalonia*, that copious amounts of olive oil were the best way to nurse a man back to health, and he did not stint on it, bringing in rich, dark, oily soups, dolma in viscous chicken stock, peppers stuffed with rice and pimiento. The first day, he'd backed through the swing doors into the ward with a basket of tepid food, an enormous bouquet, a functioning mobile phone and, most disconcertingly of all, his broken emotional voice. His words, loud and chopped, had fallen like stones on a drum.

'Ah, my friend, my dear friend, you must eat. What are they giving you? You must tell me anything you want and I will get it for you. Anything, you hear, anything!'

Pat had had to intervene to quieten his clubbing generosity, to somehow excuse him to the medical staff and to those peeking censoriously from their private rooms along the corridor.

Once, when his mobile phone had gone off, Adriano had yelled in astonishment. '*My* phone? *My* phone! My friend, forgive me.' He'd turned shortly afterwards to one of the nurses who was talking to a colleague and reminded her, 'Please, quiet for my friend.'

Someone had a word with Pat on her way out, but Adriano was not to be stopped: he had seen his visits as an inescapable obligation: 'Eat.' 'Drink.' 'Tell me what you want.' Each day of Fraser's hospitalisation, the commands had rained down upon him.

'Kaia-Lise, we have guests!' Adriano bellowed. 'Come out of the shadows. Show respect, interest. You care only about who sent you twelve red roses.'

'That's ridiculous, Dad.'

'If I catch him,' he growled.

But soon he was trying to make everything all right with her again. He approached Kaia-Lise, both hands held out as if bound at the wrists.

'Don't you touch me,' she shouted at him. And again for good measure, 'Don't touch me!'

Adriano's shoulders rose and fell as he pleaded with her in his rough, halting English. A look of hurt crossed his face, clear as a weather front, this vulnerable bull of a man in his uncultured marble palace. I could not help thinking how ridiculous he looked, an ageing but successful man brought to this whimpering state by his fifteen-year-old daughter.

The servants had evaporated to the kitchen, which lay to the left at the back of the hall. It was hard not to think that this was only a grander version of the living space of his village house in Greece.

I yawned and excused myself. Surely, it was time now to go.

'You think I'm a fool.'

I had been so involved watching everything as though it was theatre, passing the odd comment to Pat, that I'd overlooked the fact that I was part of it all. Adriano had turned to me now and his great open face looked remarkably calm and untroubled, a rogue fleck of hair plastered to his forehead.

'No, I . . .' The truth was that I didn't know what to say. I'd thought I was invisible to him.

'You think I'm a fool.' He repeated it with growing conviction. 'You see me with my daughter and you think, *the fool*. You think she is the one who will hurt me. And do you know you are right? She is the one who will hurt me.'

'Adriano, I'm really not thinking . . .' I was aware of a nerve flickering in an eyelid and the blood rushing to my face.

'I see the way you look at me tonight. You see a clumsy man from a village in Greece who has made good. That is true. That is what you see. But you do not see the hours that cost me my marriages, that make it difficult for me to be the father I want to be. The photos do not show that. The photos do not smell of sweat. I know you have done nothing like I have done, so I show you my pictures. But what do you see in them? That is what I do not know.'

Too late, I realised that the photographs, which I had thought were a diversion, an opportunity for him to indulge in a little nostalgia, to share his past with his very dear friends, had been his attempt at engagement. Having failed, he was taking another route.

'I look at you, my friend, and I wonder what have you done? What have you ever done that you look at me like this?'

I shrugged in the silence. Why didn't Pat speak now?

'Give me your hand. Your hand, give it to me.'

I tried a laugh, that came out as an exhalation, and, as if it meant nothing – no more than the pretext to a parlour trick – I held out my right hand. He turned it over and looked at it closely, rubbing with his fingers the ends of mine. I felt his large thumb press into the soft heel and palm.

'I know little about you, my friend, but your hand has no surprises for me. I think it is a simple story it tells.'

He looked up into my eyes, from below his hooded lids, and I dipped my head.

'Me, I leave my village. I shake my father's hand. Big strong hand. Oh yes, that, my friend, was a hero among hands. I embrace my mother. We do not speak. We know I am going to a world where I have to go. There is nothing for me in the village, because we all know, the young and the old, that there is not even enough work for our donkeys there. And my father knows, as only a father can know, that more than anything I need to work. I have a huge, insatiable appetite for work. Not to work the land, which is all there is for me in the village, but still, in another way, to see things grow. And, a young man, I must satisfy that – as strong as I must satisfy this.' He let go of my hand then and clutched his privates. Kaia-Lise turned away in disgust.

'Gross, Dad, just gross!' She stormed off upstairs.

But Adriano was untroubled by her. 'My mother too knows what I must do. But she says to me to remember the village. And I remember the village. I remember where I am coming from. But I know, no matter they know why I leave, how I give them pain. Pain till the end of their days. So yes, my daughter – she gives me pain. While I . . . I give her twelve red roses. And you see it as if I am humiliated. As if I am the fool. Let me put it for you like this. What you see is a man who is drowning in the sea and, as the waves lash him, he lifts his daughter onto the palm of his hand and he places her onto dry land, as far as his arm can reach. That is the important part. As far as his arm can reach onto the land he'll never find himself. But at that moment he has never felt so alive. So what you see, my friend, if you have eyes for it, is a man being alive. It is a pity for you if you cannot recognise that.'

Adriano turned to Fraser then, Fraser with his gentle face, his bulging, blueish eyes – the blind Tiresias for whom he would do anything.

'Fraser, my good friend, there are worse things than being a fool, aren't there? Fraser, you see that I am right?'

And Fraser said so softly, it was almost beyond hearing, 'Oh, Adriano, in all things, you are always right.'

PART THREE

Few Souls

—

The Memory Tree

Spreewald, Germany

In a leaden November light,
the landscape waits passively

for whatever's to come. Water
is filmed with ice. Canals stretch

into the woods like silent roads,
the black pods of upturned barges

at their sides. In an apple orchard,
trees hold up splintered hands.

A few apples have survived
windfall, survived harvest, survived

their stalks' forgetting – brassy
and unpalatable, starved of everything

but light. Other fruit was riper
and sweeter, other fruit

was not discounted by the birds;
yet these dry throwbacks remain –

as some fruit, some animals,
some homes and a few stricken people

will survive a careless army
that cuts through the dark forest

and that harvests what it chooses
from all the fires it leaves in its wake.

In Another World: *Among Europe's Dying Villages*

Andrey

I was sitting on the terrace of a bar with Andrey when three men surrounded a girl. Whatever they wanted, it did not seem to be good news for her. I could see Andrey becoming agitated and I put my hand on his forearm – it was, I thought, a situation that would right itself. One of the men looked over at us, and at Andrey in particular. The man had a face like a shovel, dead eyes. There were rumours that the Mafia was everywhere.

Those fucking guys, Andrey said, after they'd gone. Did you see those fucking guys?

Andrey was small and wiry with a large head like a puppet's. His deep eyes were set wide apart on a face as broad as that famous mask of the warrior king, Agamemnon, the eyes narrowed to almond slits.

Once he had calmed down, I asked him whether he often got into fights.

No, I fight if I have to. But I am a pacifist.

And then he told me, No one comes near me if I don't want him to. It's in the eyes. They can see it in my eyes.

Back in the village, when he was ten years old, someone had wanted to kill his father. The man had a 'shooter', but Andrey placed himself between the man and his father. And the man could see in his eyes that he had no fear.

Yes, I thought, the eyes must say, Take me on if you want to, but you are going to have to kill me, because I will fight like a cat and I will not give up.

I felt my heart go out to him then.

As communism fell and his world became chaotic, Andrey had taken to the road. He'd left his young wife, and the child he told me would be a genius, in the small crumbling concrete block with its outside toilet. He was in his mid twenties, still with small rolling shoulders and with feet light as a dancer, looking for some place that was not the village.

His eyes – that fixed gaze, the one he'd never wasted on me – had kept the world at a distance, down the many roads he would take after our short encounter. And, as the roads began to blur in his memory, so the images of his wife and son faded, though certain forest smells reminded him of the father whose life, he told me, he had once saved.

Late one night, he met one of the small packs of wolves that were thriving in the bleak interstices of a recast border. Though Andrey had looked at them fiercely, he was unable to keep them at bay. Either that, or, one night, walking the potholed strip of a road, through the black canyon of a forest, he met a timber lorry, travelling at speed. Its headlights blinded him; its force broke every string in his body. But it did not stop.

In Another World: *Among Europe's Dying Villages*

A Few Souls: The Emptying Villages of Russia

'What is in it, in this song?'
Nikolai Gogol

1

When she tells you her history,
   you see her black soil rich with blood.
She'll tell you she had happiness.
   Something you haven't understood.

Rimma didn't accuse us of being spies on our first visit. It was only after a distant neighbour told her that strangers asking such questions must be spies that she became suspicious. When we returned, her earlier cooperation had been replaced by evasiveness – a turn of the head, a distrustful glance – though not by any rudeness or aggression. She soon thawed, and, later, when her daughter telephoned, she smiled as she informed on us: 'I have *spies* with me today.'

Rimma lived in a handsome single-storey wooden house, at the far edge of the small, compact village of Kozino. Its new blue paint and green gable ends distinguished it from the silvery hue of the weather-worn wood of the other dwellings and outhouses. Beyond the village – making an island of its few houses – were gaping flat fields, sparked by dandelions in the sunshine. Kozino lay in the administrative oblast of Kostroma, roughly four hours' drive north of Moscow. This was one of the areas most seriously affected by depopulation in all of Russia; its maps were marked with the names of villages now 'uninhabited', or, as the census calls them, 'population points without population': Polovinovo, Severny, Igoshino.

Kozino, Rimma told us, had always been a small village – a scattering of twelve or so households – that had once boasted two shops and a cheese factory. There was no sign of shops or factory now, and Rimma was the village's only permanent resident. The first time we visited, a Labrador-sized dog, its chain stretching from its kennel, had barked our presence and brought Rimma, walking with a slight limp, beyond the threshold of her house. My travelling companion and interpreter, 23-year-old Masha, who I was to discover was conversant with the languages of all animals that could be stroked, nuzzled and scratched, soon silenced the dog. Chickens pecked in the dirt around our feet, and a broad-chested rooster reminded us he was not only our equal, but a little bit more besides. A ragged terrier appeared, evidently stone deaf. 'We're an old family here,' Rimma told us later, with a smile. 'All of us' – with the exception of one young black cat, which wove itself through the big dog's legs: evidently, they were great friends.

Rimma wore a blue-flowered sleeveless housecoat and her late husband's felt boots. Her own, still the colour of matt silver, stood in the inner porch, off which a heavy door led into the living room, bedroom and kitchen. The porch smelled of earth, the richly concentrated smell of soil held close to one's nose. It smelled too of that reaction between the earth and the human body when they are in intimate and prolonged contact with each other. This ante-room was where the boots, the tools and the metal churns all stayed.

Rimma's small living room was darkened by heavy wooden furniture round the walls, including a tall cabinet for the 'good' china and family mementos – small pottery and glass ornaments. In the centre of the room, opposite a large television set, stood a table with two newspapers spread on it, showing the television schedules. On the floor were saucers of cat food, dog food and milk. The carpet was engrained with the dust and dirt of a smallholding's daily life.

Rimma had come to live in Kozino after marrying a tractor driver in the collective farm. She'd been born just two kilometres away in the village of Troitskoe, had left school at thirteen and started work in charge of two oxen, delivering milk from Troitskoe to the cheese factory in Kozino. She had to load churns onto the cart. Two such churns, filled with water, sat at her entrance. She told us that the thirty-six litres of milk they had once carried weighed fifty-six kilos and the churn itself weighed twelve. Little wonder that, when one of them had dropped on her foot, she had had to give up that line of work. Next came a spell as a dairymaid in Troitskoe, before, as she put it, she went into 'trade', working as an accountant for a network of ten local shops, one of which was in Kozino; the others were in neighbouring villages.

She credited her bad knee and her eye problems to carrying such huge loads when she was so young. Nevertheless, when I tested the dead weight of the full churn, she started for it, as if to show how it could be lifted. When she smiled at my discomfort, her sly sense of humour and her intelligence shone behind her owl-like glasses. At such moments, with her short, boyish, grey hair, she seemed once more to be the young woman in the faded marriage photograph on top of the cabinet.

We moved through, past the white mass of the disused oven, to the cramped kitchen for tea. She was clearly enjoying our visit – she had reached early on for her fat photograph albums to show us pictures of the family who visited her when they could, barbecuing in summer, playing in the winter snow, but there was no complaint of loneliness. In summer, she told us, she worked the garden; in winter she knitted, read books and watched television.

'I do what I can,' she said. 'If I don't feel like doing something, I don't do it.'

When I asked why she stayed on alone here, she said, 'This is the area where I was born. I like village life. And I'll only leave the village when I'm so old that I can't do for myself.' In the way people now talk about farmers being custodians of the countryside, Rimma was a solitary custodian of village life. Yet the statement 'I like village life' seemed rather preposterous. In what ways could living in such isolation be termed 'village life', and in what ways could it be an enjoyable way to live? Then I remembered the sharpest of contrasts – Moscow.

Moscow has become many things: a city of reputed corruption and attendant violence, a city that does not know the difference between displaying its new-found wealth and flaunting its gaudiness. It is a city making up for lost time, a thrusting city for the young and for those on the cusp of middle age, a city that shows no appetite for the past or for those who come from it. On a previous visit to Russia, walking along the banks of the River Neva, I had been struck by the good fortune of my attractive, lively companion and guide, Ludmilla, to be alive at this precise moment rather than at any of the viciously inhibiting times that marked the preceding century.

'What amazing luck to be twenty-seven now in Russia.'

'It's great to be twenty-seven anywhere,' Ludmilla replied, and I thought how utterly separated she seemed to be from her country's recent history.

I could see those who weren't – the ageing babushkas, grey-faced and shabbily dressed – standing at the bus-stops with their plastic bags beside Moscow's newly fashionable women, confetti'd with all the predictable labels. Russia has over a hundred billionaires, but most of the elderly Russians survive on Soviet-sized pensions of roughly fifty dollars a week and live on bread, grains and tea. Masha told me that the young city doctors do not want to know their problems.

The shortcomings of Rimma's village life were equally clear, if more predictable – isolation, loneliness, the hardships of the seasons that city life diminishes. But she tended her cottage garden with pride and was largely self-sufficient; her pension was extra income, to spend on family presents and on the occasional trip to the city. There was also more to Rimma's 'village life' than its physical circumstances: it existed in her memory. Between the villages of Kozino and Troitskoe lay Rimma's *rodina*. The word can mean homeland on the scale of Russia, but, with its qualifier *malaia*, it becomes 'small homeland', the village and fields that are marked by their inhabitants' intimate knowledge. Covering those two poles of identification, *rodina* has strong similarities with the French *pays*. To leave your village – your *malaia rodina* – is to experience, as Aleksei Leonov describes it in his story, 'Kondyr', 'intense pain, which [is] so much like death'.

There was also a risk in uprooting herself, in crossing any threshold, whether a doorway or a village boundary: at liminal spaces, there is uncertainty – no more so than between the village and the road.

Rimma had crossed that threshold as a very young woman, when she moved the two kilometres from Troitskoe to Kozino. Her *rodina* had narrowed to this one village. But between the threshold of her wooden house and the village boundary, she could revivify the life of Kozino, and her place within it.

¶

Before she put on a headscarf and a thick woollen cardigan to show us her garden of neatly hoed vegetables – onions, potatoes, cabbage – she pointed to a board of medals, red and gold, awarded to her husband, the tractor driver. From below the photograph albums, she eased out a folder of certificates, many of which carried images of a soft, pastel-red Lenin – benign, smooth-browed, contented. They had been serially awarded for 'diligent work in the field of agriculture'. To most people now, such *realia* carry the currency of trivia – the medals have had significance drained from them; they are baubles you can buy for a few roubles on the stalls of Arbat, the touristy, trendy pedestrian street in Moscow. On a previous visit to the capital, I'd even seen Lenin on Arbat. He'd had a stick-on beard and was standing by a photo booth, waiting desultorily for customers. In the sunshine, beads of glue were dripping down his chin. But Rimma held to the history she shared with her husband, who had died three years before of a heart attack. As she took out each certificate, she shared with us her pride in a hard-working man. A blue tractor stood, like a monument, or a guardian spirit, outside her house, beside four tall birches and a lilac tree, where she chose to be photographed.

Of the changes that had overtaken her village – and of what she knew beyond it – she would only say that they were all due to politics. Her opinion now, given with a shrug, was that there were 'too many capitalists'. On the best time to be alive, she wouldn't be drawn. 'Life is life,' she said with a smiling resignation. 'Life is life.'

She watched us go, after both visits, standing well beyond her door, for, as we had learned, to linger in the threshold was bad luck. There was something of the old sea dog about her as she leant slightly forward on her stick, holding us in her sight. The last time, we left her standing in the rain, the fields dark and empty, her hens round her feet and her deaf terrier beside her.

¶

Masha was New Russia: brought up in the Siberian city of Kransoyarsk, where both her parents were journalists, she moved to Moscow to study interpreting and translating. The languages she operated in were English, Spanish and French. Since graduation, she had specialised in theatre and had already worked for one and a half years with Tom Stoppard on the Russian production of his trilogy, *The Coast of Utopia*.

She had recently returned from India, but had also worked as an interpreter or volunteer in Australia, Italy and other parts of Europe. She had turned down a job for three months on a film to be shot in Slovenia in order to be my interpreter. She told me not to worry – 'It was an action flick.' Besides, she claimed that she thought this was such an interesting project. 'For me, it's as enriching an experience as India.'

Slim as one of the birch-tree girls of local folklore, she told me she had a typically Russian face: pale skin, the slightly upward 'cut' of her eyes, the long curve of her jaw – the clean lines of an icon. An icon that could break into laughter, or a shining smile. She knew more of Russia than most. It took two and a half days by train from Moscow to visit her home town, where, as a child, she wore mittens to take exams in minus forty degree temperatures and had once had plastic bags of vodka bound to her feet to save them from frostbite. A Russian schooling had also given her a thorough knowledge of Russian classics – Tolstoy, Chekhov, Turgenev. All the major works had been part of her school curriculum.

'You know,' she told me, 'you should read Gogol's *Dead Souls*. It's the book to read while you're doing this project.'

Dead Souls tells the story of Pavel Chichikov's attempt to buy up the dead souls of serfs who have remained on the census, and, by this means, to establish his credentials as a landowner. In an essay on the novel, which Gogol preferred to think of as a *poema*, Vladimir Nabokov claims that 'it is as useless to look in *Dead Souls* for an authentic Russian background as it would be to try and form a conception of Denmark on the basis of that little affair in cloudy Elsinore'. Nabokov's opinion is bolstered by Gogol's own disparate experiences of Russia. However, these seem to me to have been sufficient to give Gogol a keen sense of Russia's immensity, for the

A Few Souls: The Emptying Villages of Russia

internal geography of *Dead Souls* is one of the book's most arresting features and carries some of its most telling poetry.

¶

After our first meeting with Rimma, we walked back through Kozino, past the small pond with the neat *banya* beside it, past the ghost pitch with its frayed remnants of a net and its narrow, three-person viewing bench, the bald basketball hoop. When we reached the main single-track dirt road, we saw a woman walking towards us, her arms held taut by four bulky shopping bags. She was heading for Troitskoe, three kilometres from where the bus had left her on the main road. Her face glistened with the sun and the effort and she was grateful when we offered her a lift.

To live and to travel in rural Russia requires, among other qualities, patience and fortitude. There is a saying that Russia has two problems: fools and roads. Gogol knew about both, and his description of the Russian countryside in *Dead Souls* has not greatly dated:

> Scarcely had the town receded behind them when the wild and nonsensical stuff that is the stock in trade of our writers began to register itself on both sides of the road: hummocks, fir-groves, stunted, scraggy stands of young pines, the charred stumps of old ones, wild heather – rubbish of that sort. They came upon villages strung out in a line, their huts looking like old woodpiles covered with grey roofs, the carved wooden decorations hanging beneath them like embroidered towels.

The comprehensive list that is eventually exhausted by its own ambition is one of the stylistic features of Gogol's book. Here, the detail eventually dissipates into 'rubbish of that sort'. It is a natural response to the vastness of the Russian landscape. What keeps the contemporary traveller focused as he travels, for mile upon mile, between tall canyons of birch and pine, slabbed with light, is the state of the road, which makes a nonsense of any computations of distance.

In Another World: *Among Europe's Dying Villages*

The only valuable measurement is of time, and one needs to have plenty of it. For mile after mile, often the only man-made structures to be seen are the bus shelters. Blue, if they have a colour, rusted if they don't. And one person, perhaps, standing fixed in a lonely spot.

'What a strange, and alluring, and uplifting, and wonderful something lies lodged in the word "road"!' wrote Gogol. Indeed. Looking, for example, down a length of road that dips for a quarter of a mile and rises for the same before it disappears over the horizon – a broad artery for an ambitious empire that would make a Roman proud – you can see that the traffic, a car and a lorry, one of those slightly amphibious, blocky Soviet ones, does not come towards you straight, but meanders from one side of the road to the other. You will also note that there is not one accepted route to take to avoid the potholes, the crumbling edges, the undressing of all that a road should be. The vehicles engage in a kind of improvised dance that could be set to music.

Except at times it is a fatal dance. Every so often, amongst the uniform green, there is a flare of colour, a garland marking where someone has died – because of carelessness, drink or the unexpected, on the usually empty roads. Outside the village of Glebovo, for example, at the junction where the lane into the felt boot factory meets the road, there was a wreath bound to a wooden stalk. Below it were the splinters of the motorcycle parts left when a timber lorry hit one of the workers at the end of his shift.

'Eighteen years old. A very good boy,' the supervisor told us.

¶

For Tamara, leaving her village to travel to Kostroma for her shopping was an arduous trip. But as the Russian countryside continues to empty, and as the harsh winters continue to ravage the road surfaces, there is less and less chance that anything will be done to improve the infrastructure of roads and transport. 'Emptying villages' is the term preferred in Russia to refer to the depopulated settlements. However, in many cases, the absolute of the Spanish

A Few Souls: The Emptying Villages of Russia

phrase *abandonado y en ruinas* is a more accurate reflection of the situation the villages are in.

As we bounced along the dirt track towards Troitskoe, Tamara waved her hand at the fields of scrub and hogweed. 'Just ten years ago, all this was crops. Crops and cows grazing. Look at it now.'

She pointed out the gable end that was all that remained of the buildings that had constituted the collective farm. We parked at a spot where the road buckled into impassable ruts and Tamara insisted that we come in for tea. Her house was 140 years old and she wanted us to see it.

We walked past the colourful cemetery, its graves on the edge of the wood, each of them within its own gated fence and containing a small table and benches where visitors could come and spend time, picnicking with the dead. At almost sixty, I was not far off the average lifespan (sixty-three years) of the Russian male. The female lives on beyond him till she's seventy-five. Drink, they say, does him in, or accidents related to drink, or diseases such as tuberculosis. A cursory look at lifespans on the small metal plates attached to the crosses seemed to confirm the earlier male deaths: one grave was fresh, a photograph of a young man standing on it, cigarette ends all around.

There was a short climb after the cemetery before we came to the first dark and dilapidated houses of the village. We dragged our legs through the tall grass, following Tamara, past the collapsing school and the houses with their small vegetable gardens tended by those who live elsewhere. The term 'dacha' may conjure a Chekhovian image of Muscovites seeking the peace of the countryside as a break from the busy life of the city. There has always been something aristocratic about the word and then later something suggestive of power and privilege. The houses that have become dachas in the Kostroma region, however, are redolent of none of these attributes. Instead, many are former family houses and gardens, maintained during the spring and the summer to supplement provisions. We are talking about necessity here – the basics a Scottish croft once provided. In 1991, when the Soviet Union collapsed and the textile city of Ivanova, three hours east of Kostroma, went into serious recession and depopulation, one third of the population was kept alive by food grown at the dachas.

Nor should the word dacha imply any of the gentrification of the countryside that 'country house' suggests. On the banks of the Volga outside Kostroma, and of course in all the major cities, rich people do spend weekends in their country houses, but the dachas in Kozino and Troitskoe often looked no different from the abandoned houses. Little was spent, if anything, on maintaining them, never mind on renovations. Troitskoe was in many ways typical of an emptying – in fact, an all but emptied – village. Its wooden houses were unpainted, their dark brown bodies sinking into the earth, some up to their 'embroidered', rotting, window frames. The roofs of some had completely collapsed; the roofs of others had metamorphosed into the carapaces of beetles and cracked as if articulated. Ragged curtains fell across milky windows. Many such villages had a small pond, clogged with iridescent green weeds, but beautiful and placid in the sunlight. A more sombre presence was the ruined grandeur of the church's bell tower, surrounded by a sea of hogweed and saplings.

Tamara had regained her energy, and she led on with purpose past the empty husks to her own dacha. Like many rural houses, the predictable geometry of a building made of logs gave way inside to a slightly improvised feel. Walls had been created that seemed temporary, their lines off-centre, reminiscent of walls a child might add to a doll's house, using flimsy pieces of card to create a bedroom where there had been none before. The house was clean, but smelled of damp – it was only recently that Tamara had opened it after its winter fastness. She put the kettle on and busily set the table with biscuits and a bowl of sweets.

'Let's wash our hands,' she said and indicated a water dispenser outside. After we had washed, we sat down on either side of the table and she urged us to add a herbal tincture to our tea. Tamara, meanwhile, continued to stand, shaking the city from her. She was a handsome woman with blonde hair tied behind her head and an energy and liveliness about her talk. She was seventy, the same age as Rimma, but she had not had the physical hardships Rimma had endured.

She had been born in Troitskoe and lived in the village until she was fourteen. At that time it had had between eighty and a hundred houses, a beautiful church and no fewer than two houses for priests. There had been sixty young people, in Tamara's estimate, who were ready to be married and as many children. As she recreated her childhood world, she often sounded astonished herself at how populated it had been, what an adventure it all was.

The village school had already closed when she was a child and she had had to walk two and a half kilometres through the woods to the nearest school. The school children carried batons to keep the wolves away, but they weren't really afraid because there were so many of them going to school. They climbed a hill on the way there and, on the way back, slid down it, sitting on their school bags. She recalled one school day in particular – the day Stalin's death was announced in 1953. Her family was one of the first in the village to have a radio. So everyone heard the announcement on the way to school. She remembered that they were all scared about losing the stability of a strong leader. It was the first dark subtext in her account of a childhood she mainly presented as carefree, as simple and bright as the primary colours of Soviet propaganda posters. Perhaps this was because the family had left the village when she was only fourteen and her memories had stayed preserved and crystalline.

There was, for example, a club in each village where you could dance to an accordion and watch movies, and, next to the church, now a black shell circled by ravens, there were benches around the well. Here, people gathered to sing and to listen to the accordion. Tamara and her friends would secretly trail courting couples as they walked home from the club.

Her mother worked in the collective farm, and her father had been a secretary in local government, so she had not had to curtail her education as Rimma had. But life was still hard for her parents. Her mother had had to get up at three o'clock in the morning to cut grass for cows in the collective farm. She finished at six and then she had to work on her own garden to pay their 'natural taxes' – the milk, eggs or vegetables the collective would take from each household. All this before going to her office job. Her parents, she said, in answer to one question, were too busy for storytelling.

But, for her, growing up, everything was 'interesting'. Her parents lived to a good age – her father to eighty-nine and her mother to eighty-five – and she herself, at seventy, was still active. She remembered everyone's birthday in the apartment block in Kostroma where she now lived. She had always wanted to do good for others. Nowadays, though, people were more reserved, and she found it difficult to get them involved in collective action, such as following a rota in cleaning communal areas of the building.

Every summer, her children left her grandchildren with her – hard work, as there had been no electricity in Troitskoe since the metal cables had been stolen from their posts. But, she told us, once she died, her children would let the house collapse. She said this without any sense of drama, just as she had outlined the former life of the village without any sense of loss, for her enthusiasm for the present, for our visit, appeared to be as great as her engagement with the past. In many ways, Tamara's narration was an example of the concept of the 'Radiant Past' that Margaret Paxson discusses in *Solovyovo: The Story of Memory in a Russian Village*.[11]

Through its lens, the positive features of the past are foregrounded, while the negative ones are screened. The Radiant Past, as Paxson describes it, is in some ways the reverse of a British tendency that gives primacy to hardship, then acknowledges the happiness to be found despite the situation: 'Aye, but we were happy, because . . .' In Russia, it tends to be the positive feature that is stressed first, then the more troubling. Thus, 'We all worked together and supported each other,' might be shadowed by, 'No one had any choice in what they did.'

In both cases, though, the Russian and the British, such recollection of the past is likely to stress a time when there was a spirit which had united people in an egalitarian way – though clearly the ideology and the cause would be different. It follows that individualism leads to fragmentation and division. Of course, the notion of the Radiant

---

[11]And in doing so, she acknowledges her debt to Kathleen F. Parthé's *Russian Village Prose: The Radiant Past*.

A Few Souls: The Emptying Villages of Russia

Past is hardly a new idea. Pushkin articulates it beautifully in 'The History of the Village of Goryukhino': 'The idea of a golden age is common to all nations and demonstrates only that people are never content with their present and, from experience having little hope for the future, they embellish the irrevocable past with all the colours of the imagination.' Tamara was not the only woman I met in the region who viewed the luminous past in this way, or who had a partial image of Soviet life as people gathering 'to sing and to listen to the accordion'. However, as Catherine Merridale has shown, in *Night of Stone – Death and Memory in Russia*, memory for those who have endured the Soviet era is problematic. It is hard to reconcile present circumstances and revelations with a time when the state decided who and what to memorialise, decided whose sufferings had import. Nor is it at all desirable to be so taken with the Radiant Past that the present seems lonely and fractured. History in Russia is indeed unpredictable; the threshold that separates the present from the past is a dangerous one, to be crossed with prayers and incantations. The women I met seemed to circumnavigate the perils of this threshold by avoiding casting clear-eyed judgment on either side of the divide.

Outside again, the village was bathed with sunlight, its grasses rich, its small flowerbeds alive with colour. Its past life – as Tamara had presented it to us – seemed similarly light and cohesive. We came across a four-year-old boy, Sacha, visiting the village with his grandmother.

'In earlier times,' he told us, with a small elegiac sigh, 'we used to have a cow.'

In Another World: *Among Europe's Dying Villages*

In Another World: *Among Europe's Dying Villages*

2

From heaven fell a little star.
It landed right on Isupovo.
It took the life of its last man,
the famous Vasily Bykov.

Karabanovo was a small village an hour's drive east of Kostroma. Again, much of it could have been described by Gogol – 'old woodpiles with grey roofs' – but there was a handsome whitewashed church with black onion domes and a handful of recently built timber houses on a track leading off from the main street. Father Georgy lived in one of these. It was Masha who had discovered him through the Hospitality Beds agency, a website that offers young people the opportunity to couch-surf and take advantage of local knowledge anywhere they choose to go. Masha had herself hosted a number of travellers in Moscow who had contacted her through the site. She had addressed the Kostroma region, outlining the project and asking if there was anyone we should meet. A reply came back that there was this 'cool priest' . . .

We rang the bell on the gate of his substantial wooden house and were told by a young and serious woman with a thick black plait that the Father had been resting. If we would follow her, he would see us shortly. We were shown into the small, warm kitchen. I noted an enormous bottle of Johnny Walker, used for water, and a tea towel with an Irish blessing pinned to the wall:

A Few Souls: The Emptying Villages of Russia

May the road
rise to meet you,
may the wind be
always at your back

Father Georgy entered. An electric hedge of white hair, given greater emphasis by the black cassock he wore, rose from its parting.

'Welcome,' he said.

'Oh, so you speak English?' I said.

'A bit. What brings you here? Sorry for being inquisitive. We get so few foreign visitors.' He spoke in soft, perfectly modulated English. We obviously showed our surprise, because he smiled – a small mouth, partly hidden by the curlicues of his beard. 'Are you hungry? Natasha will prepare you something to eat. Some potato perhaps.'

We sat round the kitchen table as Natasha silently fried small burgers and mashed potato for us.

After his shock of hair, the other thing that was striking about Father Georgy's appearance was that he was blind in his left eye – its lid drooped without ever quite closing. And the fingers of his left hand were fused, leaving him with a thumb and something that looked more like a small limb – or turkey neck – than anything resembling a hand.

'Dying villages?' he said, taking a sip of black tea. 'I could take you to twenty around here. They leave them first because there is no job that pays much – if there is a job at all – and then they leave because there is no school. Priests, for example, they don't want to come here. A small, aged congregation can't give much and – did you know a priest in the Orthodox Church can marry? Well, there is nothing for a wife to do here in terms of work. For myself, I like village life.' He paused to smile. 'I like green.'

I asked him how he survived without intellectual company.

'A friend in need is a friend indeed. Books have always been my best friends. I have a good library. Once, it used to be an excellent library. It had, for example, Pushkin's *Collected Works* from the period in which they were written. But I don't have them now.'

When Father Georgy first came to Karabanovo, the small church had only three walls and no roof. He packed two suitcases with books from his library and took them to a bookseller on the Arbat in Moscow. The bookseller, seeing the quality of what he'd brought, asked him why he'd brought the books all the way there. 'We will come to you!' They came with a truck and paid him 20,000 dollars for his books. Then they came again. He used the money to put a roof on the church and to start building another one. The church in Karabanovo was, he told us, a very ecumenical concern. He was given money for it by Lutherans and by the Irish Catholic priest who had given him the tea towel. Some of these donations were hard for his congregation to understand. For, to many of them, Orthodoxy and Christianity were synonymous. Catholics, by this reckoning, were not Christians – only Catholics. His parishioners would say to him, 'Father, Christ was born in Russia, wasn't he? The Bible is a Russian book.'

I wondered how many villagers attended his services.

'Last Sunday there were seven people at the service. Sometimes it is hard for them to get to the church without transport. Sometimes, there are only three – myself, Natasha and Alexandr, our treasurer and a former offender.' Alexandr's presence was significant, because, for Father Georgy, organised services were only a small part of his ministry. 'As a priest, charity is important to me. Of particular interest to me are two groups – ex-offenders and orphans. I mean, have you seen anyone caring about ex-offenders, orphans or old people in our government?'

He told us, in that simple way he had of disguising complexity, that he liked building things. 'In Russia, we have a saying: A man should do three things in his life – have a son, plant a tree and build a house.'

That afternoon, in addition to the church he had reconstructed in Karabanovo, he would take us to a church he was building in another village, one he was renovating in yet another and to an orphanage he was building on the banks of the Volga. Added to which, there was a new well in one village, a village whose administrative hut didn't have a national flag. So he bought one for it to fly. His building team was composed of ex-offenders. He paid them what he could and when he didn't have the money, he gave them food and tobacco. The administration gave him nothing and never had done. Through experience and conviction, and irrespective of who was in power, he had adopted Solzhenitsyn's dictum: 'Don't trust them, don't be afraid of them and don't ask them for anything.'

As a student of English and German in Moscow, he had been expelled for refusing to consider political jargon in his linguistics class. He had finished his degree in St Petersburg, as he referred to it even then, and worked as a lecturer in linguistics for fifteen years while he sought ordination. This he achieved in a village in the south, near Kursk. His suspension had followed two incidents – the first, his wearing of the cassock in public. The KGB told him it was permitted in church, but not in public places. Father Georgy could find no legal basis for this ruling, a point he made in a letter to the KGB church affairs body, a copy of which he also sent to a contact at the BBC. He was summoned to the KGB offices, where he was told he could wear his cassock in public, 'But be it on your own head.' Their hope was that some staunch communists would give him a salutary doing. It didn't happen.

The second occasion was when he had raised money for the church roof. He was told that he first had to make a contribution to the Peace Fund. Father Georgy had no problem about giving money to the Peace Fund, but he had objections about being told to do so. Again, legality was questioned; letters reached the KGB and the BBC and Father Georgy began his suspension.

He was still suspended when Ronald Reagan's visit to Moscow took place in 1988. Because he'd written a couple of articles and because of the letters that had found their way to the BBC, Father Georgy was invited to the ambassador's house to meet the American president. He told them that he was not interested. What about your wife? Even less. Your son? His son (who, at the time of writing, was vice speaker in the Israeli Knesset) said, 'Sure.' So they went together and twenty cameras filmed Father Georgy wearing his cassock.

The call soon came from the Ministry of Religious Affairs.

'Why are you involving yourself in politics? Go to your church.

That is where a priest should be.'

'I would if I had one. I have been petitioning you to be given a parish for one and a half years.'

His first parish was in a village north of Kostroma, and now he had been in Karabanovo for nine years. I asked him whether it was easier to be a priest in post-Soviet Russia.

'Oh today, particularly in our cities, the Orthodox religion is very popular, very hip. Putin and Medvedev are both big believers. You can see them at every official occasion in the Cathedral of Christ the Saviour, professing their faith.' This is the vast glittering cathedral in the heart of Moscow that was built on the site of the cathedral dynamited by Stalin in 1931. The site had remained famous as the Moskva Pool, the world's largest open-air swimming pool. No New Year bulletin used to be complete without footage of hardy, spirited Muscovites bathing among the broken ice. Private and state funds had paid for the new cathedral to phoenix from the drained emptiness.

'But . . . how shall I put it?' Father Georgy gave the light smile of a man talking of wayward, simple children. 'For example, on television, there was a broadcast of Zhirinovsky, a leader of the far right, walking round the church with a couple of his functionaries behind. He stopped before one altar. "Who's dat?"' Father Georgy gave Zhirinovsky a fitting Brooklyn inflection.

'"Saint Michael."

'"Two candles . . . Who's dat?"

'"Saint Jerome."

'"One candle."

'I prefer,' he concluded, 'to take my religion more seriously than that.'

The tea was finished and Father Georgy suggested a village not far away that might be of interest to us.

The road to nearby Ivanovskoe was constructed of concrete slabs the size of coffin lids, manoeuvred into place with metal loops. The drive was a noisy, bumpy one. For most of the journey, the forest was close to the road. In Russian, there is no linguistic distinction between 'forest' and 'wood', and though the vast repetitions of trees

A Few Souls: The Emptying Villages of Russia

that we passed through were ostensibly forest, up close, where the light reached, there was the intimacy I associate with woods. Stopping briefly, we heard the rich birdsong, saw the forget-me-nots, and the bright shafts of quivering light that fell across the silver aspens. The light on the birch bark seemed to emanate from it and to refract from one trunk to the other. Such 'aliveness' could indicate the presence of *dedushka lesovoi*, 'grandfather forest', a spirit that could take any form he chose.

Just outside Ivanovskoe, we passed the ruins of the collective farm: rows of outhouses and enormous grain stores, abandoned and decaying like wrecked ships no one cares to salvage. The largest farm, similar to the one we had explored outside Kostroma that morning, had taken farming to an industrial scale. It had had great arched entrances with signs blazoned across them: Potato Sorting, Mechanical Workshop, Animal Complex, Grain Store. As Orlando Figes explains in *A People's Tragedy*, 'The key to [the] communist utopia was the control of the food supply: without that, the government had no means of controlling the economy and society.' Collectivisation was one of the most brutally enforced changes in Soviet society and cost an estimated 10 million lives. The result was that seventy-five per cent of Russian land was bound up with the collective farm. Nevertheless, in spite of its great human cost, the *kolkhozy* were not a qualified success. In 1966, Eric R. Wolf commented in *Peasants* that 'The private plots allocated to cultivators have proved vastly more productive than the collective farms. Although constituting only 3% of the total sown area of the Soviet Union, these private holdings produce almost 16% of the total crop output and nearly half of the livestock products.'

The collapse of the Soviet Union led to the abandonment of all but a few collective farms. Lacking any state support, their electric power supplies failed and the local schools closed. Young families moved away, leaving the villages of the old. Why certain farms survived when so many others went under was a question that intrigued me.

In Another World: *Among Europe's Dying Villages*

A Few Souls: The Emptying Villages of Russia

*There are no children to harvest
their fruit, but the fruit trees don't tire
of giving. Gangs come from the town,
strip cherries till the trees are bare.*

We drove into Ivanovskoe, past the yellow mansion of the old landowners, the Birukovs, now a hospital threatened with closure, and climbed the hill to the highpoint of the village, its main junction. We parked and Father Georgy heaved himself, in his ankle-length black cassock, out of the car. There were two buildings here, side by side, looking like an argument. One of them was the utilitarian rectangle of the House of Culture, where the former Soviet state had framed the permitted entertainment and education of the masses. On the mosaic of its front wall, Vladimir Ilyich Lenin, arm outstretched, was in active and preachy mode. Running beside him were the slogans: 'Land for the Peasants', 'Workers Unite'. On the side of the building, more frivolously, a couple, in peasant costume, danced to an accordion. Many of these such buildings were still used as village halls, but there was no care expended on them. On this one, bits of mosaic had fallen off, and the old posters still advertised films from Soviet times. On a bench by its door, the handful of youths left in Ivanovskoe huddled in their sunglasses and leathers.

Standing beside the House of Culture was the other half of the argument, one of Father Georgy's building projects – a new church.

It was, at present, a basic structure, a square of logs with the rectangle of its tower rising from its centre. Father Georgy was keen, he told the three men working on it, to get the wood clad with bricks before the weather warped it.

The old church had been demolished for the House of Culture; the present one was being built on the old graveyard. Father Georgy picked up a length of white bone and, before tossing it aside, said he wouldn't be surprised if it were human. Many people had told him that he should knock down the House of Culture because people went there to drink and would urinate on the church. But why, I wondered, given the demographics – and the church attendance – was he building a new church here at all? In fact, how could he explain his avowed intent to build a new church in each village within his parish?

'Because I am a priest.'

This was an answer that came as no surprise. Blunt and factual. He had, after all, already informed us, 'I always present the facts, in personal life and in religion; you must draw your own interpretation.' He was, though, prepared to elaborate in the matter of his church-building.

'There are lots of women in these villages whose husbands went off to fight in the Second World War. They never returned. Their children went off to the cities and the women are alone. For them, the church is important as a club, as a meeting place. Women can wear new dresses there – where else can they show off a new dress? They can talk, like the way they do in shops. There are very few shops. The church is important for old people in the way that a school is important for the young. Someone will say to me, "Father, if there were a church here, maybe I wouldn't go to stay with my children in the city. If there were a church here, my children could be married in it, my grandchildren christened. I could be buried here in the village."' *Malaia rodina.*

In *The Highland Clans*, Alistair Moffat describes how important lineage was to the Scottish clans, how before Culloden, and the battles that preceded it, the clansmen had stood and recited their genealogy: 'they needed to remember them, to summon up all of the memory of their people, all of their ancient prowess'. The concept of *rod* – of lineage – is at the heart of *rodina*, and ideas of ancestors and intercession, suggested by Moffat's description of Highland bloodlines, are also reflected in the concept of *rod*.

As for the rare display of new dresses, if the spiritual bar seemed set low here, it was not something that concerned Father Georgy, who claimed to have no interest in imposing his faith on anyone, a type of faith that was slightly disarming in its pragmatism, given his vocation: 'I like reciting the liturgy. I can't explain why. It's just something I like to do. Since communist times, I've despised propaganda, even religious propaganda. I don't like miracles. I believe in being rational.' His views were underlined on another occasion: 'If ever you meet anyone who tells you they know why children suffer, don't believe him. Spit in his eye.'

He led us now to a house with a large vegetable garden leading up to the main road. He had brought us to meet Lydia to talk about village life. Lydia was seventy-two, bustling and energetic, with a long plait wound round her head and a flowery housecoat. She was in a state of nervous excitement as we sat down at the small kitchen table.

'Oh Masha,' she said, 'I don't even know how to put down spoons properly!'

She cut a cake, laid down a bowl of chocolates. The good china was produced and wiped with a cloth. We passed round a cup to feel its lightness on our palms. She cleaned small glasses and poured a sweet homemade wine of cherries, currants and forest berries from a half carafe. She drank hers quickly and said, 'Whoa, that's better,' in a simulacrum of relaxation. But when the tea was in the pot she leant towards it, placing one hand on top of the other, as if in fear something trapped inside it might escape. Was it the presence of the priest, Masha or the foreigner – the first to be welcomed at her house – that was making her so nervous?

She poured the tea and bounced up again to reach for a large jar of cherry jam, all of which she tipped into a bowl. I watched as Masha spooned it directly into her mouth. Once, twice, thrice. Such manners! But, I learned later, this was *varenie*, not a jam for spreading – it was too loose for that – but for spooning into your mouth, while drinking tea. Honey was taken in the same way.

Lydia settled briefly like a bird, and Father Georgy waved a hand to signal we should begin to ask our questions. During our conversation, he sat side on to the table, a black profile with white detail, his blind eye giving no clue as to whether he was listening or dozing. In the front passenger seat of our car, slumped within his cassock, his octagonal priest's hat somehow holding down his hair, it was also his blind side that was exposed. I sensed he enjoyed the ambivalence it created – first the appearance of sleep, then the deformed hand would rise and, with a few chosen words, reality would be redefined. The black-clad profile recalled James Whistler's portrait of Thomas Carlyle, *Arrangement in Grey and Black, No. 2*. But more than this, I was reminded of those ethnographic paintings of the nineteenth-century artist, Ilya Repin, who gave Russia images of itself to which it was unaccustomed – prisoners in Siberia, threadbare peasants. Repin's gaze was unremitting, exposing his subjects in a way that could make the viewer feel slightly voyeuristic. It is, however, a gaze Father Georgy would have met with indifference, neither welcoming it, nor turning from it, as he had not turned from the KGB, from the plutocrats who replaced them or from Masha or from me. 'Ask and I'll answer any question. But make them hard ones. Bring who you want – journalists, television crews, they are all welcome here.'

Whatever state of somnolence he was or was not in, Father Georgy let Lydia tell her story without interruption or comment.

¶

Lydia's parents had come from a neighbouring village that no longer existed. She was born in Ivanovskoe and had lived there all her life. Her parents had had memories of the days of the landowners and the peasants who worked for them. 'All the villages around were owned by the Birukovs then.' Lydia had worked in the kindergarten for forty years. A desire to please and to satisfy appetites for learning must have made her a much-loved carer. At its height, the kindergarten had had seventy-two children. The main employment in the village was the flax factory, which had been built by women, as there were few men left after the war. Logs were floated down the Volga; women stood up to their waists in water, directing the logs to be carried to the factory. It was perilous work, as there were strong currents in the river, and there were many deaths. There were 230 workers who worked in three shifts in the factory. The factory work was hard; the working conditions were very poor, with bad dust and draughts. Almost no one who had worked there was still alive. It was, though, Lydia told us, a happy time. Life was hard, but they 'lived it lightly'. People then were kind and full of compassion. That was, she said, a 'peculiarity of those times'. If someone had a sick child, for example, people would look after it while the mother worked her shift.

In those days, everything was expressed in songs – grief, happiness and loss. You put all your soul into song. At family gatherings round the table, they would sing together. They also sang on the way to work. They used to sing very beautiful songs when the women went into the fields, wearing white shawls and simple dresses. Some went barefoot, some in short rubber boots with a rake over their shoulders. Again, those pictures from the Radiant Past, expressed with re-imagined pleasure.

Women would drop by in the evening and sit on the bench by the lilac tree and sing *chastushki*, the short folk songs that were so popular. Now no one sings. She knew a man who used to play the accordion back then. '"Go on," she told him, "bring your accordion. Play for us." But he was too shy with all the tape machines. Now there's no general happiness. People don't walk along the road, singing or playing an accordion.'

I asked her if she would sing a *chastushka* for me. She put her hand to her mouth to stifle her giggles, suddenly girlish. 'I can't remember a single decent one!'

'I'll go out,' said Father Georgy, rising. 'A priest shouldn't listen to such things.'

With her eyes on Masha, Lydia sang her *chastushka* quickly, in a light, breathless voice, just reaching its end before giggling. It was an innocent song, Masha told me, about a girl burning the letters of a former lover in the oven:

I flung a stack of old letters,
one by one, into the oven.
I watched the fire take them, line
by line, dreaming of my lover.[12]

She sang another one she considered daringly political, which compared Brezhnev's haircut to a piece of birch bark. She raced even faster through this one, the nerves of social memory and official disapproval still active. Stalin had, after all, condemned Mandelstam to the *gulag* for comparing his moustache to a pair of cockroaches.

[12]This is, more or less, a literal translation of the *chastushka* Lydia sang for us. The poems that punctuate this essay are derived from certain aspects of the *chastushka*, including its brevity and its assertion of values that are in opposition to those of the city. However, they make no attempt to capture the formal qualities of rhythm and rhyme that make the *chastushka* memorable. The examples of political *chastushki* are all taken from Y. M. Sokolov, *Russian Folklore* (translated by Catherine Ruth Smith).

A Few Souls: The Emptying Villages of Russia

Requests to hear a *chastushka* drew the same sly, knowing smiles from all the old women I met. Many claimed they only knew indecent ones, and one old woman dodged the challenge by telling us, 'These teeth aren't for singing anymore, only swearing.' *Chastushki* are often compared to limericks for their memorability – four rhythmic, rhyming lines – but actually we have no equivalent in our culture. It was a song so widespread that it was easily adapted for the dissemination of revolutionary belief:

> I will buy a portrait of Lenin
> and put it in a little gold frame.
> He brought me out into the light,
> ignorant peasant woman that I was.

In one of Moscow's subway stations, where there are heavy bronze representations of Soviet life, there is a statue of an earnest peasant woman, book open on her lap – one of those 'brought into the light'. At one point, Russia's rural experience was central to the Soviet project – the Russian girl/mother/worker became an iconic figure as country life was brought within the ideological sphere:

> There are no rustic lads anymore.
> This is the way we have decided the question:
> there is no village, there is no countryside,
> there is only the prosperous collective farm.

Nonetheless, as Margaret Paxson explains, the *chastushki* had limitations as political propaganda tools: 'cozying up to authority is perfectly out of character for this genre and would be roughly the equivalent of using American rap to get people to vote Republican'. The *chastushki* that lived on the tongue – and that live in memory, news that stays news – could not be coerced. However, in singing an obscene one, in the Soviet period, you risked arrest.

¶

When Father Georgy returned, Lydia had composed herself, but her lingering excitement was vented in a burst of action.

'Masha, plug that light in,' she asked, and she was soon bent over the kitchen floor before us, raising a trapdoor. She disappeared down steps into a dimly lit glow and returned with two large jars of locally picked mushrooms – one for the Father and one for myself. Like the berries that made the liqueur and the jam, the mushrooms were signs of the beneficence of the forest. These gifts did not mark the end of the visit, however, merely a punctuation. So again, we settled.

Her memories of each of the political periods of the Soviet Union were clear and acute. No one in a village was immune to the vagaries of political decisions from distant Moscow, and if the overall ideology and structure were monolithic and inflexible, with each leader came a different tone and emphasis.

Khrushchev's time had been full of directives. At that time, each villager had to pay a natural tax. If, for example, you grew gooseberries, you would have to bring a certain weight of them to the collective farm. Others might bring a specified number of eggs or quantity of milk. You would work on the collective farm in the day, then go home to work on your own acreage. Once, Khrushchev forbade people to mow hay for their own cow.

Brezhnev's term, Lydia said, was the best, because there was greater calmness and stability. Also, what impressed Lydia was that he knew how to greet people – he kissed everyone, even men, on the lips. In the latter's time, the natural tax eased. People were allowed to mow for themselves and keep two cows – a resonant number given that, in the time of collectivisation, someone with two cows could be seen as a *kulak* – a bourgeois peasant – and could be transported away or killed. In other words, cows meant wealth.

Everything went wrong in the nineties, according to Lydia. After the fall of the Soviet Union, laws were non-existent; people didn't receive wages or pensions for months. They needed the two cows, because without them they wouldn't have been able to survive. When the situation calmed, Lydia gave up her cow.

A Few Souls: The Emptying Villages of Russia

(In fact, during our trip, we met only one woman who kept a cow: Nina, from the village of Leontievo, near Kozino. The cow's name was either Little Beauty or Little Daughter. 'I'll tell you anything,' I remember Nina telling us, 'except where my cow is.' (Though Masha, who must be right, told me I'd imagined this.)

'It's hard work,' Nina had told us, 'keeping hay, feeding, milking. Young people don't want the work.' Nor is there the incentive for older people that there used to be. Pensioners used to have free travel into Kostroma, so they took their dairy produce – cheese, butter and curds – into the city to sell. Once they had to pay their own bus fare, their marginal profit disappeared, and so did two thirds of village cows. Lydia argued that it was in the Russian nature not to work if they didn't have to, though people of her generation had little option.

Before we left, Lydia wanted to show Father Georgy her 'red corners'. These are spaces in the house, or the shop or the factory, where icons are kept and where, at one time, pictures of Lenin would have been placed:

> From one window to another
> I have moved the flowering plant
> so that there might be light on the portraits
> of Lenin and Stalin.

But, just as in the village where Father Georgy's small churches were reversing the Soviet cultural centres, so in the most intimate and charged places in the house icons had once again displaced the former state's iconography. Lydia's house had two 'red corners': one high up in the kitchen with two or three small icons and a larger one in the sitting room in which four icons of saints and the virgin and child were grouped around a jam jar with a flowering twig. The house had been built by Lydia's husband, a carpenter, to whom she referred constantly as 'the master'. She pointed out the ornate window frames, which had been brought from her grandparents' house in another village and were 150 years old.

'Here, Masha,' she said, with another burst of frantic energy, 'I have

In Another World: *Among Europe's Dying Villages*

given *you* nothing.' And she broke off three small branches of white lilac to make a bouquet for her.

¶

She began to walk through the woods,
back to where her old village lay.
In a clearing, they found her lost;
her village, up sticks and away.

'There is one more place that might be of interest to you. Do you have the time?' The time needed was not specified, but soon, on a broad, dirt road, Father Georgy asked me casually if I had enough petrol. Again, distance was not specified. We made it to a village on the banks of the Volga, where we followed Father Georgy's dusty black habit along a red, rutted track to a fine large building he had intended as an orphanage.

We found three sunken-cheeked ex-offenders there. One of them had a wall, in his small room, that was a blaze of icons and candles. A man, according to the Father, in need of the utmost support.

'What you must never do,' Father Georgy had told us, 'is to give them money. Because first they'll buy a beer. Then a bottle of vodka. Then cleaning fluid.'

Still, it was a beautiful house they had built to Father Georgy's design. He told us, with that mixture of humility and self-awareness that made Masha and me wide-eyed, that it had been a straightforward task. 'Logs, six metres long, cut this way, then another set six metres long, placed the other way. And so on.'

¶

Earlier, on our journey to this village of Novobely Karenin, on a rise of the dirt road, we stopped at a graveyard with its usual efflorescence of wreaths. Before it was a handsome cross.

'We put it there,' said Father Georgy. 'I often come up here and

A Few Souls: The Emptying Villages of Russia

say prayers. Over there,' he indicated an empty field, 'used to be a large village. And on the other side too. Now nothing. You know why many villages disappeared? Sometimes, the administration would decide large villages were better; sometimes small villages. So an official would come and tell you to dismantle your house and move. Everything would be moved – lock, stock and barrel. Oh, you needed a sense of humour in Soviet times.'[13]

On our next visit to Lydia, she would tell us that the decision was not quite as arbitrary as Father Georgy had outlined it. Rather, villages were distinguished in terms of ones that had prospects and ones that didn't. If your village was in decline – if, say, many children had left home and only old people were left – or if there was little work there, the village would be moved to where there was work. The policy – *ukrupnenie* – was, in other words, a state-controlled programme of rationalisation. And it also allowed economies in the supply of electricity.

From the graveyard, I could look down the road from where we had come and to where we had to go. I turned a full circle, my eyes looking out over the idle fields, and returned to the only sign of human presence – the graveyard. This was a landscape, as Gogol has described it in *Dead Souls*, both 'desolate and splendid'. Its defining feature was absence – and absence is not emptiness, but loss. If the taskscapes of Western Europe are becoming ever sparser, here, there was nothing. Enormous landscapes with no human activity. In Bulgaria, which only experienced communism in the post-war period, it has been easier to reconnect with a life of the land. When I was there, every morning, I saw horse-drawn carts, loaded with labourers and a plough, heading for the fields. There were shepherds with their flocks and squads of women in headscarves clearing stones from the fields.

[13]There is a wonderful moment during *Homecoming*, the BBC documentary about Solzhenitsyn's train journey across Russia in 1994, after 20 years of exile. Solzhenitsyn, looking wistfully across a lake at a village, declares, "Ah, they really knew where to put a village in those days." In the abandoned village of Isupovo, I saw clearly the numbering of the logs that had made reassembly so straightforward.

Whereas here, there was nothing. A waste of fields, not 'set aside', but abandoned by history and with no activity to take the place of what had been, apart from the very occasional ploughed patch, never larger than half a football pitch. And absent villages – or villages rotting and sinking back into the earth. There were no suggestive still lifes such as the ones that can be found in the abandoned villages of Italy or Spain, the Morandi windowsills with dusty bottles and old glass globes of wine. In this climate, and with wood as the main material, nothing lasts. And the existence of many of these villages has been so temporary that there is little of the evidence of the human presence David Craig still finds so readily in the Highlands of the clearances, *The Glens of Silence* – 'the furrowed ground, [. . .] the stone walls, the lintels still in place, [. . .] the wells and ditches and other small traces which are the almost indelible features of a way of life.'

In this empty landscape, this particular Glen of Silence, Father Georgy – because he is a priest – was busily planting churches, wells, crosses and orphanages.

¶

People from the city have bought
the old horse farm. See the horses!
Their ribs move beneath their matted coats.
Horses? Crops like any other.

Tamara had been very keen that we visit a horse farm at nearby Medvedki, on the opposite side of the main road from Triotskoe. She had told us it was beautiful and that we should not miss it. Once, no doubt, it had indeed been beautiful. But now, its prime buildings shared the same sense of abandonment as the villages that had once served it. The main stables – long, low, barracks – stood not far from a low gatehouse and a ruined mansion with tall pillars that recalled a grandeur long gone. The façade at the centre of the stables, subtle as a bouncy castle, had been painted clumsily in eggshell blue. There was no one about, as usual, so we ventured inside the stables. The stalls

A Few Souls: The Emptying Villages of Russia

were a depressing sight. Heavy with horse manure, many of them had broken floorboards.

In a couple of stalls, we found a nervous horse, wild-eyed, stamping, its ribs showing through its unbrushed coat. We walked along a corridor to the wooden domed exercise area and stood in the sunbeams, admiring its faded grandeur.

Back outside, a passing woman, wearing an old t-shirt and tracksuit top, told us that the mansion had been destroyed only three years ago, and that it used to be a kindergarten. The gatehouse had once been a bakery. There was a local dairy farm of two hundred cows and calves. It was state-owned, but paid wages only spasmodically, so they had to keep selling cows to pay staff.

The decline had taken place between ten and twenty years ago. Once, around Troitskoe, you can't imagine, she said, every field was used. There was organisation and structure. Twenty years ago everything fell apart. Now they produced only milk here. The horse farm was run by Muscovites. There were two hundred horses for horse-racing or to sell to gypsies. The way the farm was run showed, Masha told me, Russia's attitude to animals – the main thing was to obtain something that could be sold. Horses, like anything else, were seen as a cash crop.

We thanked the woman for her time. 'Nothing,' she said. 'I would be glad to have something to boast about, but there is nothing.'

And at times, even the little they had was not safeguarded. An old woman in Medvedki told us that people came from the towns at night and stripped their orchards of apples, plums and cherries. Some of these would have gone to waste, others not. But there was no one to defend them.

Suspicion of Muscovites appeared to be common in rural Russia. In Medvedki, we heard of a grand Muscovite plan to reinvigorate local agriculture, but their schemes were discussed with as much scepticism as hope. The suspicion and the distaste of course went both ways. The Russian villager has been condescended to by metropolitan cultural centres since the great move to the cities began – although, at the end of *Anna Karenina*, Tolstoy brings Levin to live 'in the very holy of holies of the people, the depths of the country'.

However, in the twentieth century, in the 'time of stagnation' between Khrushchev's period in power in the sixties and the coming of *glasnost* in the 1980s, writers of Village Prose (*derevenskaia proza*) gave expression to the primacy of the village as the home of the Russian soul – but a home that was, increasingly, an abandoned mausoleum. In *Russian Village Prose*, Kathleen F. Parthé explores the senses of nostalgia and fearfulness that animated these writers: 'If the past of Village Prose is full, radiant and complex, the present is experienced as a time of loss, and the future is seen as a cultural and moral vacuum.'

Parthé identifies three major themes in Village Prose: the theme of Childhood (the archetypal story of loss), the theme of Return, wherein a villager experiences memory and change on return to their childhood home, and the theme of Uprooting, as old villagers are compelled to abandon their villages, the sites of their roots, memories and traditions. For Parthé, 'the long road' (*doroga dlinnaia*) is an image of the slow passage through the Russian countryside, but also of the journey back to the writer's village childhood, a particularly useful idea in relation to the concept of Village Prose.

Solzhenitsyn's novella *Matryona's House* is one of the first examples of the narrative of Uprooting. It ends with this judgment on Matryona, the embodiment of the selfless virtues of Russian village life:

> None of us who lived close to her perceived that she was that one righteous person without whom, as the saying goes, no city can stand.

> Nor the world.

The argument is that the Russian village represents the country's moral core – its death threatens the spiritual life of the country. By this reckoning, Rimma and Lydia would have been seen by the Village Prose writers not only as custodians of village life, but, like Matryona, as custodians of the Russian soul.

¶

If there were a villager or a peasant from this region who was emblematic of the mythic Russian 'soul', then it must be the folk hero Ivan Susanin. There is a huge statue of him in the centre of Kostroma, spade-bearded, with a staff in his hand, one of a host of images of the visionary, self-sacrificing peasant, who gave his life to save his country. Susanino, a local hub town for a number of dying villages, was named after him in 1939. The renaming was clearly symbolic, as the deed for which Susanin is remembered occurred in the Troubled Times of 1612, when Russia, lacking leadership, and with several rival claimants to be tsar, was under threat of foreign invasion.

For all its longevity, Susanino felt like a frontier town. There were the terrible pot-holed roads, the haphazard melding of substantial official buildings such as the government offices and the church with the hastily erected new living quarters. What marked it out as a centre more than its shoddy buildings was the handful of young women pushing prams. The church itself had been given over to an exhibition of Ivan Susanin and the Romanov family. In the nearby village of Domnino, where a monastery now stands, was the site of the house where Michael Romanov (1613–1645), the first of the dynasty, had lived with his mother, a nun.

Domnino was also where Ivan Susanin had lived, and, close to it, a sign pointed towards 'The Place of the Great Deed'. It was here, at the site of a huge memorial boulder, that Ivan Susanin offered to lead the invading Polish army to Moscow. Instead, he led them down into the swamps, where they and he all perished. Paintings back in the exhibition in Susanino, depicting the moment the Polish realised they had been duped by Susanin, had shown the Great Deed happening in winter. The museum held a display of a number of others – men, women and children – who, down the years, had similarly played the hero and guided invaders to their deaths. We scrambled down the hill from the boulder and walked through sunlight saplings, along duckboards lined up across the bog.

But the more impressive, slightly chilling thing to do was to stand at the top of the escarpment and look out over the landscape, the scrub stretching to the plain, to the horizon. Until you reach the Ural Mountains,

Russia is formed of the East European Plain. It is a geographical feature of little variation – pine forest, tundra or *taiga*, steppe.

When, sometime later, we drove south from Kostroma on our way to the shabby old capital of Alexandrov, where Ivan the Terrible had had his walled palace, I stopped on a narrow country road to consider the landscape. It was composed of huge fields – 'fields beyond the eye's grasp', as Gogol describes them – with no sign of human activity, grasses flattening in the wind. There were the scumbles of distant trees. And then, there was the sky, the enormous sky with clouds like ruins – dark and sun-shot – passing through the blue.

Silence.

Crows.

Robert Louis Stevenson, in *The Amateur Emigrant*, wrote that the first settlers on the American Plains often hallucinated that they were either expanding to fill the space or shrinking within it. For these settlers, of course, such a landscape had been a novel experience. Villagers in this region of Russia, however, have grown up within this unforgiving environment, in which the human dimension is dwarfed. As Maxim Gorky put it in his story 'The Dead Man', 'Invariably the steppe makes one feel like a fly on a platter.'

Of course, what Ivan Susanin thought he was defending – his understanding of Russia – was limited, but he saw it enshrined in the figure of Michael Romanov. Through him, the peasant apprehension of what Russia meant was combined with a higher conception; the invader was defeated by local knowledge. And local knowledge was often – well into the twentieth century – all the villager had.[14] As Father Georgy pointed out to us, many of the inhabitants of villages like Karabanovo and Ivanovskoe had lived all their lives where they had been born. In the Soviet period, they were tied there. With no documents, they would have been able to visit Kostroma for only a day,

[14]In Susanin's case, not only is his courage emblematic, but also his intimate knowledge of his *rodina*. 'When peasants combine to fight an outside force, and the impulse to do so is always defensive, they adopt a guerrilla strategy – which is precisely a network of narrow paths across an indeterminate hostile environment,' writes John Berger in the introduction to *Into Their Labours*.

A Few Souls: The Emptying Villages of Russia

but not to stay there. Moscow would have been a distant dream. For many villagers, the limits of their knowledge would have extended only to the next village – which could be some distance away. Don Gifford's 'edgeless universe' lay a long way away from here, and would fill most villagers with existential terror! In fact, when finding our way along minor roads south of Kostroma, we were often told, 'Go to the next village and then ask.' Masha told me that 'And then ask' was a common way to round off directions in Russia.

On the other hand, an old man in Leontievo told Masha to 'Fuck off' when she approached him, and I was grateful to him that my view of villages should not be sentimental or nostalgic. In Leontievo, the cow-owning Nina had told us, news arrived from Moscow with the men who drove there to work in the building industry. Working there, living in cramped rooms, was the only way that they could continue to live some time in the village. The news of the economic disparities they brought back must have spread some despair and resentment among the villagers. Of those who had remained, Nina told us it was not drink that killed the men, but hard work – working from seven in the morning till eight at night, then coming home to look after their own land. This was what led to their terminal exhaustion. That said, in a short space of time, four of the men we sought directions from were the worse for wear from drink.

Masha was unused to rejection. She returned through the drizzling rain from speaking to the old man with furrowed brow. 'I'd like to show him where the crabs spend winter,' she said. And whatever that meant, I knew from her delivery that it wasn't pleasant.

4

She's sitting on the old green bench
   by the side of the lilac tree.
Oh, the songs she once sang here!
   The thought of them still makes her blush.

When we returned to see Lydia, she spoke to Masha with some excitement.

'The first time you came, I didn't ask what the capital of Scotland is. If it was Canada, I would have said Ottawa. If you'd asked me the capital of Scotland I wouldn't have known. But the capital of Canada is Ottawa.'

The back-story to this trivial pursuit was that, in 1974, Lydia had been in a queue in Moscow, in the days when if someone saw a queue they joined it. Someone had tapped her on the shoulder and said, 'Excuse me, Madame.' The intrusion had caused Lydia a considerable shock, because in those days you only addressed people as 'Comrade'. She worried about who might have overheard and about why she had been singled out. The person was from Canada, which appeared to be all he had been able to communicate to Lydia, who, for her part, repeated to him all her school knowledge of Canada: 'Ottawa. Ottawa. Ottawa.' Now she was earnestly trying to perfect her pronunciation of 'Edinburgh. Edinburgh. Edinburgh.'

She also had *chastushki* ready for us. She sang them quickly, always to the same tune. Some were slightly racy.

Oh what an interesting girl I was.
I had a baby by a stranger
and then got married
as an honest woman.

Others were suggestive, though the suggestiveness of the following *chastushka* was initially lost on Masha.

I was walking, walking, walking
and found a fir-tree cone.
I warmed it by a stone
and it started jumping.

And one was more than suggestive in Masha's frank translation. Though her tone, as she gave me this translation, played with its inherent ambiguity:

I was walking through a forest
and saw a miracle under a fir tree.
A pretty girl was patching her "skirt"
with a long, thin needle.

Lydia giggled between each *chastushka*, which were all directed, through a screen of hands, to Masha. She swept the words from her mouth like something she didn't want to be caught with. She was demonstrably more relaxed without Father Georgy, yet still she indulged in some nervous saucer-shuffling with Masha, who was holding in her laughter, as they laid the table for tea. When the tea was ready, Lydia showed us how the noblewomen used to pour tea into their saucers to make it last longer.

I was interested to know how people had changed after the collapse of the collective farms.

'It's not the collective farm that's changed everything. It's history. It's war, the losses suffered in war and the fear that war might begin again.'

Lydia was seven when the war ended. Her father returned from the war without one leg. But many did not return. There was great hunger, she told us, in 1947. People had nothing to eat but old potatoes they dug up in the fields from previous years. These and grass.

'When you went to the well for water, one woman would ask the other, "How's the girl?" "Still sick," would be the reply, "lying at home." But war was what everyone feared the most. Even hunger was better. People who'd returned from war said, 'Let there be cold, hunger, but no war.'

Masha told me later that the concept of having had 'a good war' was unheard of in Russia. The Russian losses in the Second World War were truly staggering, and historians such as Tony Judt have argued that they help to explain Russia's reluctance to involve itself in foreign wars, in contrast to the willingness of the Americans. Catherine Merridale, in her magnificent and heart-breaking *Ivan's War: Life and Death in the Red Army 1939–1945*, sums up the Soviet losses:

> [. . .] the total number of Soviet lives that the war claimed exceeded 27 million. The majority of these were civilians, unlucky victims of deportation, hunger, disease or direct violence. But Red Army losses – deaths – exceeded 8 million of the gruesome total. This figure easily exceeds the number of military deaths on all sides, Allied and German, in the First World War and stands in stark contrast to the losses among the British and American armed forces between 1939 and 1945, which in each case amounted to fewer than a quarter of a million.

As Stalin put it succinctly, accounting for the Allied victory: 'The British provided the time, the Americans the money and the Russians the blood.'

These were losses on such a scale that they were felt acutely across the Soviet Union, even in this northern region, which had never been invaded. Nevertheless, the privations and fear had bred a comradeship that, according to Lydia, had not survived the fall of the Soviet Union.

'Our feelings after 1991 became acute; friendliness and warmth died out. For example, I'm the sixth child in my family of seven. If my father told us something, no one would contradict him. In those days, if someone came, my father said, "Lay the table and call the relatives." All that you had would be put on the table. Today it is different. If a brother visits his sister, no one would know. Today people are less close, less hospitable, out for themselves. Everyone has kindness in them. But today it's less obvious, it's not for the world. Today it's expressed in a different way. Everyone has kindness, but doesn't show it. We don't have universal love for each other – kindness, warmth, eagerness to help.

'For example, at one time, if someone suffered a fire, everyone from the village would bring something. If someone suffered a misfortune, people would bring the best thing they could, so that people would know this person gave this and it would be meaningful. Nowadays people only give money.'

Lydia's voice, as she gave us memories that were often painful, lowered; her swollen hands were more open than on our previous visit. But these were memories from the time when she had told us, 'The times were hard, but we lived them lightly.' How did she manage to keep bright memories of hard times? Were there any good things?

'Well, good things, I can't say so. But there was *dushevnost*.'

Dushevnost is another one of the 'untranslatables'. Its root is *dusha*, the soul, and it carries the meaning of having warmth in your attitude towards people, warmth that includes the prospect of unselfish help. It is part of the egalitarianism that features in the Radiant Past. As I write, Gogol is once again at my shoulder, advising, 'There is no word so sweeping, so torn from under the heart itself, so bubbling and quivering with life, as the aptly uttered Russian word.'

'Oh, but there are good things about any time,' Lydia said. Masha noted later – as we sat in the car, reconstructing the exchanges we'd had – that Lydia's vocabulary was local and particular, that she used archaisms that would not be heard in Moscow. At times, she gave language the sense of a fable or of a proverb, with a weightiness that Masha compared to what one might come across in Homer's *Iliad*. It was a quality also identified by Catherine Merridale, when she was interviewing a peasant woman in the act of remembering: 'The men that she so skilfully conjured for me are no longer ordinary peasants. In her account, they are more like the heroes of a Russian epic tale.'

'Every age has its own advantages,' Lydia contended. 'I can't say there were only sweet dreams in those days. Nor, today, are we flying on wings. Every time is rich in something. One needs to live a life, one needs to have *one's own* experience of life to know what a life is, not learn it through someone's opinion.'

In a soft voice, with her hands clasped on the table, Lydia followed her thoughts through. 'You can't compare different times unless you've lived through those times. You can't judge by hearsay, only by your own experience. And a life of experience teaches you not to judge. After all, you can't choose when to live.'

I asked her if today's children faced challenges. Here, judgment was given free reign. '*Niet. Niet. Niet.*' She shook her head and chopped her hands through the air. 'Today's parents give everything they have to their children. I can remember my own two children. I gave them everything, but I expected something in return. Nowadays, children get the best clothes, food, everything.' She was twisting and twisting a sweet wrapper now. 'In those days, the ones we've been talking about, children had to help cut wood and fetch water. Now everything is given; nothing's expected. There is no respect for adults. My grandson comes to see his aunt in the next street, but wouldn't visit his grandmother.'

Before we left, she sat on her bench by the lilac tree and sang us one last *chastushka*. She wished us *blagopoluchie*, another of the great untranslatables, which conveys the sense of warmth (again) and prosperity in your home. A prosperity that has little to do with money.

Before we said our goodbyes, Masha went to use the toilet – a hole in the ground with a spotless lid placed over its top. Without Masha, Lydia and I stood, bereft of language, looking towards the house, up the garden to the small church and the obsolete House of Culture. Lost in a silence between us that seemed unbearably unnatural, I turned to her and, to her utter bemusement, began to sing 'Flower of Scotland'.

5

Unless you've grown old and useless,
  The village life is not for you.
Have you seen my city lover?
  Her milky hands are just for me.

On the following Sunday morning, we went to the morning service at Father Georgy's church in Karabanovo. The Orthodox service is a dramatic affair, full of choral chanting and response. Instruments are banned, so much is asked of the human voice. Father Georgy was hidden behind a screen for much of the time, then appeared with a dramatic frisson. Some churches, Father Georgy told us, employ professional singers, but he liked to sing himself and so wanted the worshippers to learn to sing too. The congregation consisted of about ten people, though just six were left for the high point of the service – the communion. As they waited for Father Georgy to offer them the host – the mixture of bread and wine in a silver spoon shaking in his hand – they did not so much form a line as curl around him, this tiny congregation of believers from dying villages in the vastness of Russia. After the separation from their priest at the start of the service, this moment of intimacy was immeasurably moving.

Afterwards, we drove to another small village, which had 'two years left to live', according to Father Georgy, where he was to officiate at a christening. As we bounced along the earthen road, the huge brass font rolling in the boot, I put to him the suggestion, made by Solzhenitsyn and the writers of Village Prose, that the village was Russia's soul.

'No, I do not agree with any of that. I don't like anything that says Russia is unique. Russia is the same as any other European country.'

'So what will be lost,' I asked, 'if Russia loses its villages?'

'Agriculture.'

After the christening, at which we complete strangers were welcomed into a private house, given prime spots on the sofa in the small living room, for a ceremony attended only by family members, Father Georgy elaborated on his views of agriculture.

'People realise that what you grow yourself tastes better – onions, carrots, potatoes. I have a friend who comes to the village for milk for his dog, because it won't take anything else. People are always saying that poetry and liturgy are dying. But it is not so. This form of agriculture – that has lasted seventy years or so – will die, but another form will survive and our village be resurrected.'

In the village where the christening was held, he had met Victor, a chairman of the collective farm, and invited him to talk to us about why some collective farms survived when so many others didn't. Victor was a stocky, balding man with a heavy moustache, and he had spent his life in agriculture. He sat astride his chair and waved a curt refusal to be photographed or recorded.

'Farms survived because of the individual qualities of the heads, their entrepreneurship and the connections they had, whether they could get good deals in terms of supplies. The head would say to the work force, "Stick in, three hard years and we will survive." The farms failing led to the villages failing. Out of nine villages, three might survive. Muscovites buy land now, but they do not have the patience for farming. Also, there is not enough labour now to support some of their schemes.

'Oh yes, the times of the collective farms were more interesting than today. We had 800 cows, seventy-five tractors, forty different machines. Within the farming complex, there were four brigades. Mostly, people stayed in the villages unless they were called to the complex.

A Few Souls: The Emptying Villages of Russia

'There was a lively social life. Competitions between brigades – football, amateur arts clubs, trips. Foreign trips to Hungary, say, or around Russia. Professional trips to neighbouring regions. But post 1991, structures failed, so the social events failed, because there was no one to check that they were taking place.'

Victor's only criticism of 'former times' was that everything in the collective farms reflected the collective belief throughout the Soviet Union – 'a collective hypnosis', as Father Georgy termed it – that people were working together and living for a better future.

'Is it sad,' I asked him, 'for someone involved in farming all his life to see land unused?'

'Yes, it's sad. But we have hope.'

'Hope,' Nikita, a visiting priest, commented good-naturedly, 'hope doesn't work in Russia.'

Victor, though, was pinning his faith on directed projects like horse-riding and the specialist breeding of beef cattle – aurochs. I can only think that Victor was using auroch as an indicative term, for the breed itself became extinct in 1627.

¶

I am, as I said earlier, close to the life expectancy of a Russian male. Around these villages, I had seen only a few men, and a proportion of these had been the worse for wear. The women are in their seventies now. Many of those villages, like a large number I visited elsewhere in Europe, have only ten years of life left in them. In fact, in his introduction to *Into Their Labours*, John Berger forewarned: 'In Western Europe, if the plans work out as the economic planners have foreseen, there will be no more peasants within twenty-five years.' And he wrote that in 1990.

How then did Father Georgy see village life in ten years' time? Typically, he would not answer. 'I am not a prophet. If you want to know what village life will be like, perhaps you should speak to my neighbours.' This was the Father Georgy we were coming to know, the gentle hand shaping our journey: first the damage, then the solution.[15]

¶

Towards evening, we approached Father Georgy's neighbours – three couples retired from the police and the army. They had just finished work for the day. In the Soviet period they had worked in a collective garden. But at that time they had been given only a small piece of land and they had had to clear it of trees. It was better here; here they had more freedom. It was while they had been looking for a suitable piece of land that they had met the Father. He had secured the plot for them. They had built handsome wooden houses and worked the land into a sizeable vegetable garden. We were shown around with pride, then we gathered at a trestle table set out with bread, cheese, bacon fat, pickled fish, pickles and vodka. Because I was driving, I didn't drink, but I raised my cupped fist in a toast and mimicked throwing my drink down my throat. I thumped my empty emptiness down on the table and this seemed to give them satisfaction enough.

Sergei, the most voluble of the group, hunted bears, though he was quick to point out that he had never shot any. His bear trips took him 200 kilometres north of here, where the villages were even more isolated.

'It all started going wrong in Khrushchev's time,' Sergei told me. 'Farmers were not allowed to farm their own land; they had to pay the natural taxes. People lost enthusiasm for farming. The decline started in the sixties and ended in the nineties. Now, you can find a whole village without one apple tree. People are not used to working their own gardens.

'The question of the future is a big question. It depends on politics. No one is pushing a rural agenda with enthusiasm. Putin has some understanding, having come from a village himself, but no clear policy.

[15]Meeting Father Georgy was a truly memorable experience. I once told him he was as close to a great man as I'd ever met. 'Yes,' he replied, without missing a beat, 'that is what Pope John Paul said to me.'

A Few Souls: The Emptying Villages of Russia

'There is the problem, for example, of the division between collective farm land and state land. State land can be bought and sold, but not collective farm land, no matter how unused it is. We would like to expand, buy a couple more fields, but it is impossible to do so.'

Nor, Sergei told me, was it particularly good land. I'd noticed this earlier on the trip, when, negotiating a waterlogged track, I'd slipped one foot into wet, clinging, clay. Orlando Figes commented, in *Natasha's Dance*, on the heroic efforts the peasants had to make to meet the quotas demanded by the aristocracy of the region to maintain their ostentatious lifestyles when the yield from the soil was so poor. By contrast, the black soil of the Ukraine was so rich that the German army had shipped it in trainloads back to Germany.

'Would people come if land were available?'

'Sure. Why not? They'd come for pleasure. We are all from the village. Not this village and not even from a real village. But from a village of people.'

I had been focusing all the time on Sergei's face, his lively eyes, his glinting, gold-capped teeth, as Masha simultaneously translated what he was saying, softly and fluently. On an earlier occasion, with Lydia, I had found myself confused, my focus wavering as, attempting some kind of misguided politeness, I turned from Lydia's Russian to Masha's translation and lost part of both. Language is more than simply the words, which is why Gabriel Garcia Marquez advises journalists to abjure note-taking and recording equipment during an interview for keen attention and an awareness of how voice and gesture give words their nuances. Now, towards the end of the trip, I think Masha and I had 'flow'.

¶

Oh little apple and whither
    are you rolling? Ever further
from the riverside, where she waits,
    as still as a heron, for you.

Oh little apple, will this be
   your last word? There are no last words.
The river flows on, as it must,
   past you and the lonely heron.

'We are all unique,' asserted Father Georgy, when he refused any special pleading for the Russian 'soul', and it is true that all countries have a historical heritage and legacy to which they must answer. The reasons for the abandonment of villages in Russia are in some ways different from those in other parts of Europe – more extreme, more calculated – but also, in the centuries' long drift to the cities, broadly similar. If the effects are the same, so are the questions elicited: What can be done to encourage people to stay in the village? How might others be persuaded to join them?

When I first envisaged a trip to Russia, I wrote to a contact in Moscow who had translated some of my poems. She had replied angrily – or perhaps defensively: what did I hope to find there? She suggested there would be nothing but lonely old women and drunks. What would be the point? How would I talk to these people?

Well, who can predict anything at the start of a journey? I have never been a prophet of my own life, following mostly what has held my interest. But who could have predicted what I would find in dying villages in Russia? Whatever it was I did find, it had nothing to do with dying. Instead, I returned from my trip with some of the strongest testaments of how to live a life.

The qualities necessary to survive in a dying village are resilience, self-sufficiency, independence, a sense of humour, and a feeling of rootedness within a value system that is under constant threat. I don't know whether these are qualities that the people I met – people like Rimma, Tamara, Lydia and, of course, Father Georgy – had in abundance to start with or whether they had developed them over the course of their determined way of life. During my Russian journey, I thought often about Rimma's assertion, 'Life is life'. In one sense, out of context, it has the superficial weight of 'That's life', as Frank Sinatra swings it. Or else it carries the spuriousness of the *'sic vivitur'*

A Few Souls: The Emptying Villages of Russia

of a Latin primer. Its weight, its real authority, comes only from who is saying it and from the experiences that have given it its true, if hidden, shape.

Rimma's rites of passage have involved her in the history of her empire, her country and her village. Her acceptance of what has happened to her has safeguarded her from any embitterment. But I believe that something more profound lies below the surface, that each 'life' is coloured differently, both far from static, both in a constantly changing relationship with each other. The first may encompass the traumas of change she has endured, or perhaps it may be that from its upheavals the Radiant Past flares now and again. In this particular equation I catch a ghostly 'still' appearing – life is *still* life – so that the second 'life' represents all we can know and all the possibilities of being alive that are open to us: the love we feel for our partners, our children, the sun on the forest leaves. It is of this life that poetry speaks. Living alone in her empty village, there is therefore something both heroic and deeply moving about Rimma's, seemingly off-hand, deeply earned, 'Life is life'.

Gogol wrote *Dead Souls* as an exile in Italy. From the glory that was Rome, he wrote: 'Rus! Rus! I see thee, from my beautiful far-away, thee I see: all is poor, scattered and comfortless in thee.' This is where I must part company with my literary companion – for when I think of those threadbare communities, poor and scattered, 'from my beautiful far-away', it is with a memory of concentrated warmth and openness, a generosity born of experience, not stripped away by it.

In Another World: *Among Europe's Dying Villages*

Afterword: Raasay

Between the village and the road:
*   a moon of golden broth*
*   shining in the darkness,*
*   a pinch of earth for remembrance*

On returning from my travels, I began working with artists and craftspeople I knew to give physical shape to some of the responses to what I had seen. When I had gathered together a number of these response-objects, I put them inside what I called the 'Suitcase of the Dying Village' and took it on the road.

My friend Erlend told me I was like a *colporteur*, a peddler of religious books in nineteenth-century France. I found an image online of a man weighed down by a suitcase of printed material hanging from a strap around his neck. I told Erlend that I liked the idea of the travelling, but that dissemination of tract or dogma was far from my desires. I wanted to engage with people round a table, sharing with them my thoughts, poems, recordings and objects – in return for their own reactions, opinions and memories of village life.

In one workshop at Sabhal Mòr Ostaig, the Gaelic college on Skye, a student indicated the horse's bit from my suitcase. 'Everyone in Skye has one of those. They find them and don't know what to do with them. They don't want to throw them out because they are still functional; only they have no function.'

I had worked with ceramicist Archie McCall on the creation of a double of the horse's bit. This one was made from porcelain and was ghostly, light, fragile. A third one had also been fashioned. It too was made of porcelain, but had been broken into pieces, its edges worn smooth like the old sheep bones that had lain around the croft where I found its original years ago. I placed the trinity of horse's bits on a piece of green felt on the table.

The student explained that the ubiquity of the bit was emblematic of the fact that at one time every village would have had a blacksmith, as central to the life of the community as the church minister and the schoolteacher. Who would have guessed then that the way of life centred on the horse would prove to be so fragile? Alexander Nicolson's collection of nineteenth-century Gaelic proverbs lists, in its index, three proverbs relating to 'husband', seventeen to 'house', twenty-two to 'wife' and forty-one to 'horse'. And just four generations later, the intimacy we shared with these creatures has become the preserve of the tiniest minority. Yet their detritus still seeds the earth – a symbol, like so much else in village life, of the passage of time.

At the same workshop, someone had asked me, pointedly, 'Do you live in a village yourself?' It was a fair question to ask of someone writing about villages.

'No,' I had said. 'But, then again, yes. I would say that the street I live in is a village. There are enough people in it with a shared interest in each other to make it one.' A number of people nodded their heads at this, agreeing that it was one of a number of working definitions of what a village may be.

My friend Alastair Reid maintains that the village is the perfect human organism. His partner, Leslie, once told me she had asked him if he had been to a particular street outwith Greenwich Village, where they have lived for many years.

'What?' Alastair had replied. '*Beyond* 14th Street?'

Interestingly enough, no matter where we are born, if someone asks us to draw a map of our childhood (as I have often asked people to do in creative-writing classes), that map will look like a village. For all that, I thought about the student's question later, and I wondered whether one might have asked of someone such as Doug Saunders, who has written about shanty towns in megalopolises in a variety of world cultures, whether he lived in a city. 'No,' I imagine him replying. 'But one of the interesting things I discovered is that these enormous shanty towns are in fact composed of interlocking villages.' In fact, it's possible *not* living in such a city would be an advantage in writing about one, given that the writer would be able to observe its idiosyncrasies and challenges more objectively.

Perhaps my own initial unease with the question reveals something about our relationship to the village: that we often imagine it to be tight, in-growing, opaque, the opposite of the preening, declarative, but shallow, city. And there is perhaps a subtlety in the villager's awareness of his surroundings. As Kathleen F. Parthé notes, everyone in a village portrays and is portrayed. This dual perspective may lead to a more nuanced or mindful set of relationships than the city fosters. Although, as the poet Meg Bateman, a resident of Tarskavaig on Skye, pointed out to me, there is always the flipside: she would be reluctant, for example, to push an argument with a fellow villager to its full conclusion in the way she would, without hesitation, in the city. Sustainability runs through all aspects of village life.

¶

Still life, or the life of the object, with its emphasis on the transient or the outmoded, is one of the obsessions that has lasted this journey with me. So too is the sense that an affinity with the human scale of the village runs deeply within us, no matter where we might live. It is, I think, such a sense that gives the image of the village and its counterpoint, the road, their resonance.

As I have written elsewhere in this book, the road has an ambivalence of meaning for the village. It carries both the prospect of excitement and the potential of threat. A well-maintained or new road can be a vital force in sustaining the livelihood of a community. It can also enable people to leave, just as it may bring the world to their doors. The power of the road as metaphor, and as reality, has brought me, finally, to the island of Raasay. In a number of ways, Raasay answers, as do many Highland islands and communities, the diminishing narrative that tugged at me when I first read of Villabandin – although Raasay's story, like that of many other communities, is shot through not only with abandonment, but also with carelessness, cruelty and a sense of loss so powerful that we can imaginatively apprehend the complex of emotions that accompany such sites. In the second half of the nineteenth century, roughly fifty per cent of the population of

Raasay, 500 to 600 people, was cleared from the south of the island to accommodate sheep. 'The window is nailed and boarded/ through which I saw the West,' Sorley MacLean wrote in 'Hallaig', a poem that has come to memorialise all the cleared villages.

For all that, here on Raasay, there is a road, the significance of which seems to avoid all ambivalence. A monument to its maker declares:

> This former footpath to Amish – a distance of 1 3/4 miles – was widened to a single track with passing places and prepared for resurfacing by Malcolm MacLeod BEM (1911–1988) South Arnish.
>
> He completed this work single-handedly over a period of ten years.

It means little to read about these 1 3/4 miles without seeing – on a morning of driving rain – how the road twists and climbs and plunges across the landscape. 'Where folk's fate is to go, ford or hill won't prevent,' states a Gaelic proverb. The road's creation is a feat of the utmost resolve, skill and ambition; it is the tale of a hero's doings, justly celebrated in *Calum's Road* by Roger Hutchinson. (As I write, an adaptation of the book for the National Theatre of Scotland is currently touring Scotland and will end its run in Raasay Village Hall.)

However, 'ford and hill' were not the only challenges to the building of the road. As great an obstacle were the vagaries and failures of the Highlands and Islands Regional Council, to which Calum asserted that his scattered community – his clachan – in South Arnish did not count. Roger Hutchinson captures the great differences between the council's and Calum's own aspirations:

> Council bureaucrats and engineers [. . .] saw nothing but a bumpy, dusty track to nowhere. Calum saw children playing and old ladies enjoying the autumn of their lives in Arnish, Umachan, Torran and Fladda. [. . .] Calum knew what Hebridean ghost towns looked like; he walked through them every week. He was determined that his beloved South Arnish would not share the fate of Umachan and Kyle Rona.

It is not surprising that, in his later years, Calum became very interested in those who had left his island, to travel across the seas to new worlds, such as the one where, in a coffee shop on the Prairies, my story first began. Calum MacLeod had historical vision for the long and for the short term. And yet there remains a world of difference between the South Arnish of today and the vivid description of coastal village life that Tomás O'Crohan gives in his *Island Cross-Talk*:

> The fish were lifting their heads out of the water, the birds singing their music and on land the people were stripped to their shirts, re-earthing the potatoes. Groups were coming down both sides of the hill with bundles of furze and children raced east along the slope after morning school. Smoke was rising from every house at this time – dinner on the way surely.

If I am to be honest, I have no real sense of *rod*, of lineage, of whatever stretches beyond my grandparents. And even then, having known only one of them, my awareness is fractured at best. Nevertheless, I find myself drawn to the ideas embodied in the resonant words of this journey – *hiraeth, ionndrainn, pays, rodina, rod.* Something in the dying village has stirred up in me a nostalgia for a rooted sense of community and fellow-feeling. These are feelings that have been answered and shared with many of those I have met. It may be that a sense of the village is hard-wired into us all. Perhaps it is this that has brought me onto this wet, grey, wonderful road, and to this final thought that, whatever means are being sought to revitalise or to reinvent village life, there are, all over Europe, people living mostly in isolation, caught in a slip of time between action and elegy, facing their future with resilience, resignation, stoicism – and, as one group of villagers wishes me to assert, affection for the meagre present and the rich past.

Raasay, October 2011

How to Tell When a Village is Dying

when she wishes she had
written down the recipe
as her mother never had

✴

when no one thinks the world
starts from there
anymore

✴

when there's a bird
in the baptismal font,
bird-shit on the altar

✴

when the vigilant light
in the window
goes out

✴

when, if there were a ship,
it could not be launched;

*

when if there were a ceilidh
there would be no reels

*

when the hole for the cat
is a hole for mice, spiders,
wind, leaves and snow

*

when the silence
behind the faded curtain
grows like a crystal
when the basketball hoop
spells O against the wall

*

when the village girls
            have no eyes
for the village boys

*

when a cauliflower – white,
firm and perfectly weighted –
is beyond the care of language

＊

when the most common
greetings become thick
with significance

＊

when the village doesn't fit
            the villagers' dreams –
in the spaces: darkness   keening

＊

when the summer corn
rots in the fields

＊

when the sheep carry
their best wool into winter

＊

when he follows his sons,
tramping across the potato drills –
the new shoots risen

＊

when he feeds his dog,
but leaves his belly empty

✳

when the sea closes over an isthmus
that can only be crossed
one way
when the village is a language
rarely spoken

✳

when someone asks:
is that a dog or a wolf,
a grain or a weed?

✳

when she keeps a few things
packed to give herself
the option

✳

when the old graves
and the freshest graves
wear the same face

✳

when he recalls the priest
closing his mother's eyes:
what will his dead eyes stare at?

✳

when she remembers the band
playing in the village square,
but forgets the war it ended

✳

when he wonders what
his children think of him:
it's not him his children think of

✳

when he catches the dog
in a corner, weeping

✳

when a village can be trodden on
like a puff-ball, emitting
the same smoky breath

✳

when the forest presses on
the outskirts: in time
it will march up the main street

✳

when you walk through the silence
with no stories to tell

✳

when they bless the road
that brings them anyone

✳

when his hands are strangers:
monstrous, thick-skinned, scarred

✳

when the summer pastures
are unvisited: the mountain berries
rot, once birds have had their fill

✳

when they gather names
that sound like a song,
a lament

✳

when someone decides that,
on the newest road signs,
the name should be omitted

*

when fists are deep in the basin
and the water quiet and the moment
lasts till eternity
when assez! bastante! assente!
enough! and the tines of the fork
quiver in the earth

*

when

when

when

when

when

when a bird sounds
like a baby crying

List of Images

All photographs were taken by Tom Pow.

In Another World: *Among Europe's Dying Villages*

Sources and Further Reading

Rafael Alberti, 'Primero y secundo cuadernos chinos (1979–1982)' in *Versos sueltos de cada día*, Alianza Editorial, Madrid, 1999

Clive Aslet, *Villages of Britain*, Bloomsbury, London, 2010

Margaret Atwood, *Survival: A Thematic Guide to Canadian Literature*, McLelland and Stewart, Toronto, 1972

Gaston Bachelard, *The Poetics of Space* (trans. Maria Jolas), Beaon Press, Boston, 1969

Alex Barclay and Tom Pow, *The Ae Project* (film with accompanying booklet), CREATE, Dumfries and Galloway Council, 2010

Michel Bélivier and Benoît Sadry, *Oradour sur Glane: Regards et histoire*, La Maison d'Oradour, Oradour sur Glane, 2007

John Berger, *And Our Faces, My Heart, Brief as Photos*, Writers and Readers, London, 1984
Into Their Labours, Pantheon, New York, 1992

Julia Blackburn, *Thin Paths: Journeys In and Around an Italian Mountain Village*, Jonathan Cape, London, 2011

Hugh Brody, *Innishkillane: Change and Decline in the West of Ireland*, Penguin, Harmondsworth, 1973

Norman Bryson, *Looking at the Overlooked: Four Essays on Still Life Painting*, Reaktion Books, London, 1990

Camilo José Cela, *Journey to the Alcarria* (trans. Frances M. López-Morillas), Granta, London, 1998

Anton Chekhov, 'Peasants' in *The Kiss and Other Stories* (trans. Ronald Wilks), Penguin, Harmondsworth, 1982

CIA World Factbook, available online at *https://www.cia.gov/library/publications/the-world-factbook/* (updated annually)

Alain Corbin, *Village Bells: Sound and Meaning in the Nineteenth-century French Countryside* (trans. Martin Thom), Columbia University Press, New York, 1998

Council of Europe, *Recent Demographic Developments in Europe 2005*, Council of Europe, Strasbourg, 2006

David Craig, *On The Crofters' Trail*, Birlinn, Edinburgh, 2010

David Craig and David Patterson, *The Glens of Silence: Landscapes of the Highland Clearances*, Birlinn, Edinburgh, 2004

Iain Crichton Smith, 'The Village' in *Collected Poems*, Carcanet, Manchester, 1992

Robert Darnton, 'Peasants Tell Tales' in *The Great Cat Massacre and Other Episodes in French Cultural History*, Penguin, London, 2001

Norman Davies, *Europe at War 1939-1945*, Macmillan, London, 2006

Roger Deakin, *Wildwood: A Journey through Trees*, Hamish Hamilton, London, 2007

Directorate General for Regional Policy, *Regions 2020, Demographic Challenges for European Regions*, Commission of the European Communities, Brussels, 2008. Available online at *http://ec.europa.eu/regional_policy/sources/docoffic/working/regions2020/pdf/regions2020_demographic.pdf* (accessed 18 January 2012)

Richard Ehrman, *The Power of Numbers: Why Europe Needs to Get Younger*, Policy Exchange, London, 2009

Orlando Figes, *A People's Tragedy: The Russian Revolution 1891–1924*, Jonathan Cape, London, 1996

Natasha's Dance, Allen Lane, London, 2002

The Whisperers: Private Life in Stalin's Russia, Penguin, London, 2008

Don Gifford, *The Farther Shore: A Natural History of Perception, 1798–1984*, Faber and Faber, London, 1990

Nikolay Gogol, *Dead Souls* (trans. Robert A. Maguire), Penguin, London, 2004

Maxim Gorky, 'The Dead Man' in *Through Russia*, The Echo Library, Teddington, 2006

Elena Gorokhova, *A Mountain of Crumbs: Growing Up Behind The Iron Curtain*, Windmill, London, 2010

Robert Hébras, *Oradour-sur-Glane: The Tragedy Hour by Hour* (trans. David Denton), Les Chemins de la Mémoire, Honfleur-Saintes, 1957

Ernest Hemingway, *By-Line: Selected Articles and Dispatches of Four Decades*, Pocket Books, New York, 1998

Eva Hoffman, 'The New Nomads' in *Letters of Transit, Reflections on*

Sources and Further Reading

Exile, Identity, Language and Loss (ed. André Aciman), The New Press, New York, 1998

Roger Hutchinson, *Calum's Road*, Birlinn, Edinburgh, 2006

Tim Ingold, *The Perception of the Environment: Essays in Livelihood, Dwelling and Skill*, Routledge, Oxford, 2000
Lines: A Brief History, Routledge, Oxford, 2007

Pierre Jourde, *Pays Perdu*, L'Esprit des Péninsules, Paris, 2006

Ryszard Kapuściński, *The Other*, Verso, London, 2008

Declan Kiberd, *Inventing Ireland: The Literature of the Modern Nation*, Jonathan Cape, London, 1995

Laurie Lee, *As I Walked Out One Midsummer Morning*, Penguin, London, 1969

Carlo Levi, *Christ Stopped at Eboli*, translated by Frances Frenaye, Penguin, London, 2000

Tim Lilburn, 'How to be Here?' in *Living In The World As If It Were Home: Essays*, Cormorant Books, Toronto, 1999
'Philosophical Apokatastasis: On Writing and Return' in *Thinking and Singing: Poetry and the Practice of Philosophy*, Cormorant Books, Toronto, 2002

Julio Llamazares, *The Yellow Rain* (trans. Margaret Jull Costa), The Harvill Press, London, 2003

Federico García Lorca, *The House of Bernarda Alba* in *The House of Bernarda Alba and Other Plays* (trans. Michael Dewell and Carmen Zapata), Penguin, London, 1992

George Lovell, 'The Solitude of Solanell' in *Geographical Review*, Vol. 86, No 2, 1996

Norbert Lynton, *William Scott*, Thames and Hudson, London, 2004

Iain Gordon MacDonald, Chris Ryan, Bill Lawson and Gregg Wagstaff, *Touring Exhibition of Sound Environments* (TESE), Earminded, 2002

Alasdair Maclean, *Night Falls on Ardnamurchan*, Birlinn, Edinburgh, 2001

Sorley MacLean, *Collected Poems*, Polygon, Edinburgh, 2011

Derek Mahon, 'New Space' in *An Autumn Wind*, Gallery Press, Dublin, 2010

In Another World: *Among Europe's Dying Villages*

Sara Maitland, *A Book of Silence*, Granta, London, 2008

Catherine Merridale, *Ivan's War: Life and Death in the Red Army 1939–1945*, Faber and Faber, London, 2005

Czesław Miłosz, 'A Treatise on Poetry' in *New and Collected Poems*, Allen Lane, London, 2001

O. V. de L. Milosz, *L'Amoureuse Initiation*, André Silvaire, Paris, 1998

Alistair Moffat, *The Highland Clans*, Thames and Hudson, London, 2010

Caroline Moorhead, *Human Cargo*, Chatto and Windus, London, 2005

Vladimir Nabokov, *Lectures on Russian Literature*, Mariner Books, New York, 2002

Peter C. Newman, *The Company of Adventurers*, Penguin Books, Toronto, 1985

Alexander Nicolson, *Gaelic Proverbs*, Birlinn, Edinburgh, 2006

Tomás O'Crohan, *The Islandman* (trans. Robin Flower), Oxford University Press, Oxford, 1977

Island Cross-Talk (trans. Tim Enright), Oxford University Press, Oxford, 1986

Seán Ó Faoláin, *An Irish Journey*, Longmans, Green and Co., London, 1941

Catherine Merridale, *Night of Stone: Death and Memory in Russia*, Granta Books, London, 2000

Kathleen F. Parthé, *Russian Village Prose: The Radiant Past*, Princeton University Press, Princeton, 1992

Margaret Paxson, *Solovyovo: The Story of Memory in a Russian Village*, Woodrow Wilson Centre Press, Washington, 2005

Walter Perrie, 'Exilics: Leaving Lochboisdale, 1919' in *The Edinburgh Book of Twentieth-century Scottish Poetry* (eds Maurice Lindsay and Lesley Duncan), Edinburgh University Press, Edinburgh, 2005

Paul Preston, *¡Comrades!: Portraits from the Spanish Civil War*, HarperCollins, London, 1999

Alexander Pushkin, *The History of the Village of Goryukhino* from *Tales of Belkin and Other Prose Writings* (trans. Ronald Wilks), Penguin, London, 1998

Alastair Reid, *Inside Out: Selected Poems and Translations*, Polygon, Edinburgh, 2008

Outside In: Selected Prose, Polygon, Edinburgh, 2008

Graham Robb, *The Discovery of France*, Picador, London, 2007

Mar Roman, 'Withering Heights', *Edmonton Journal*, 12 March 2006

Doug Saunders, *Arrival City*, William Heinemann, London, 2010

Jay M. Smith, *Monsters of the Gévauden: The Making of a Beast*, Harvard University Press, Cambridge, Massachusetts, 2011

Y. M. Sokolov, *Russian Folklore* (trans. Catherine Ruth Smith), Wildside Press, Rockville, Maryland, 2011

Alexander Solzhenitsyn, *Matryona's House and Other Stories* (trans. Michael Glenny), Penguin, London, 1971

Andrzej Stasiuk, *Fado* (trans. Bill Johnston), Dalkey Archive Press, Champaign and London, 2009

Robert Louis Stevenson, 'An Autumn Effect' from *Essays of Travel*, Chatto and Windus, London, 1920

Travels with a Donkey in the Cévennes and The Amateur Emigrant, Penguin, London, 2004

J. M. Synge, *The Aran Islands* (ed. Tim Robinson), Penguin, London, 1992

George Thomson, *Studies in Ancient Greek Society: The Prehistoric Aegean*, Lawrence and Wishart, London, 1949

Gillian Tindall, *Célestine: Voices from a French Village*, Sinclair-Stevenson, London, 1995

Leo Tolstoy, *Anna Karenina* (trans. Richard Pevear and Larissa Volokhonsky), Penguin, London, 2011

Giles Tremlett, *Ghosts of Spain: Travels through a Country's Hidden Past*, Faber and Faber, London, 2006

Eugen Weber, *Peasants into Frenchmen: The Modernization of Rural France, 1870–1914*, Stanford University Press, Stanford, 1976

Jason Webster, *¡Guerra! Living in the shadows of the Spanish Civil War*, Doubleday, London, 2006

Eric R. Wolf, *Peasants*, Prentice-Hall, New Jersey, 1996

In Another World: *Among Europe's Dying Villages*

www.dyingvillages.com